Lost in the Yellowstone

NEW EDITION

Lost in the Yellowstone

"Thirty-seven Days of Peril"
and
A Handwritten Account
of Being Lost

TRUMAN EVERTS
EDITED BY LEE H. WHITTLESEY
FOREWORD BY TOM TANKERSLEY

THE UNIVERSITY OF
UTAH PRESS

Salt Lake City

The Defiance House Man colophon is a registered trademark of the University of Utah Press. It is based on a four-foot-tall Ancient Puebloan pictograph (late PIII) near Glen Canyon, Utah.

19 18 17 16 15   1 2 3 4 5

LIBRARY OF CONGRESS CATALOGING-IN-PUBLICATION DATA

Everts, Truman, 1816-1901.
  [Thirty-seven days of peril]
   Lost in the Yellowstone : "Thirty-seven days of peril" and a handwritten account of being lost / Truman Everts ; edited by Lee H. Whittlesey. -- New edition.
     pages cm
    ISBN 978-1-60781-429-0 (paperback : alkaline paper)
1. Yellowstone National Park--Description and travel. 2. Everts, Truman, 1816-1901--Travel--Yellowstone National Park. 3. Explorers--Yellowstone National Park--Biography. 4. Missing persons--Yellowstone National Park--Biography. 5. Wilderness survival--Yellowstone National Park--History--19th century. 6. Search and rescue operations--Yellowstone National Park--History--19th century. 7. Yellowstone National Park--History--19th century. 8. Yellowstone National Park--Biography. I. Whittlesey, Lee H., 1950- II. Title.
  F722.E93 2015
  978.7'52--dc23

                                              2015005901

Printed and bound by Sheridan Books, Inc., Ann Arbor, Michigan.

CONTENTS

FOREWORD

DURING THE SUMMER OF 1870, Truman Everts entered Yellowstone as a member of the Washburn-Langford-Doane expedition. He stated that the many "marvelous" and "strange" tales about the region had provoked his curiosity to explore it. Little did he know of the historic legacy he would leave or that his own marvelous and strange story would become so entrenched in the literature of Yellowstone. Truman Everts's "Thirty-Seven Days of Peril" is one of those compelling tales that needs to be saved and read by each generation. It is the account of a lost, nearsighted, inexperienced woodsman who travels confusedly for more than a month over fifty miles of the Yellowstone wilderness, an adventure filled with fluctuating drama, humor, and suspense. Each day for thirty-seven days, Truman Everts, an unlikely hero faced with seemingly overwhelming obstacles, has to reach within himself and find the resources and will to keep going.

The Yellowstone wilderness is a harsh and unmerciful environment that contrasts with and enhances its unparalleled beauty. It was created by the cumulative effects of cataclysmic and dynamic

geological forces. Today we have our own associa-
tions with the place, and we share with it a much
different relationship than did Everts. But, if we
are somewhat familiar with nature and the Yellowstone landscape, we are likely to understand
the adage that "nature is not gentle." Shortly after
the park's establishment, Thomas E. Sherman,
son of General William T. Sherman, while viewing the Yellowstone Plateau, wrote, "Society in
general goes to the mountains not to fast but to
feast and leaves their glaciers covered with
chicken bones and eggshells." While it may have
been Truman Everts's desire to feast in Yellowstone wilderness, it was not his fate.

Since the creation of Yellowstone National
Park in 1872, Yellowstone has become a part of
this nation's character. While Yellowstone is a
place where we can go to refresh our minds and
renew our spirits, today over three million visitors
come to this great park annually. And while most
of us share some inspirational relationships with
Yellowstone, we rarely experience it alone. As we
explore Yellowstone's awe and wonder, we are
rarely a stone's throw away from civilization. Our
physical needs have been taken into consideration,
possible extenuating circumstances have been calculated for us, and thus the National Park Service
protects us from the park. For most of us who
visit Yellowstone today, various traumas of the
Yellowstone experience might be illustrated by
long lines at fast food restaurants, by the deplor-
able condition of the park roads, or by the poor
timing of Old Faithful's next eruption—all of
which throw us off our tight schedules. Because

most of us travel through the park on a road system, chuckholed as it may be and long as it may take, it is difficult for us to realize that we have only experienced about two percent of the park. Just beyond the roadsides and boardwalks is the Yellowstone that Truman Everts experienced—true wilderness.

While the definitions of a wilderness may vary, Yellowstone fits most of them. Wilderness might simply be defined as a large, wild tract of land covered with dense vegetation and forest. However, Webster's definition of wilderness reflects Truman Everts's experience: "Something likened to a wild region in its bewildering vastness, perilousness, or unchecked profusion." For those that have hiked Yellowstone's backcountry, Webster's definition and Everts's descriptions will sound familiar. The tangle of fallen lodgepole pines at times still causes disorientation to the most experienced hiker. The sounds of wild animals in the night can still send chills down the spine. The dangers here are inherent, because Yellowstone is indeed vast, perilous, and unchecked.

Those familiar with the literature of the park are quick to cite Everts's "Thirty-Seven Days of Peril" as the most compelling Yellowstone story ever told. Dealing with one misfortune after another, Truman Everts takes on the Yellowstone wilderness—one on one. His worldly possessions and keys to survival are essentially limited to an opera glass, thistle roots, and grit. In publishing this edition of Truman Everts's dramatic Yellowstone experience, Lee Whittlesey has three motives: first, to keep the story alive; second, to put the story into the context of 1870; and third, to provide some insight into Truman Everts himself, before and after his experience. In all three intentions Whittlesey has done a splendid job.

On a personal note, upon reading this story in the comfort of my home, I naturally thought that if I were facing such a situation that I, too, might have the courage, resourcefulness, and overall toughness of a Truman Everts and thus could survive such an experience. But after consideration, I recognized a simple, humbling truth: nobody else has ever been lost and survived thirty-seven days in Yellowstone.

Tom Tankersley
Assistant Chief of Interpretation
Yellowstone National Park

ACKNOWLEDGMENTS

My THANKS GO to Aubrey L. Haines, the eminent Yellowstone historian, for saving me from making key errors and for the map of Washburn party campsites. Yellowstone Park Senior Editor Paul Schullery has continued to offer his general support by reviewing my manuscripts. I must also thank Rocco Paperiello of Billings, Montana, whose scrutiny and suggestions keep me on my toes. Our debates are always spirited and useful, and they help me get things right.

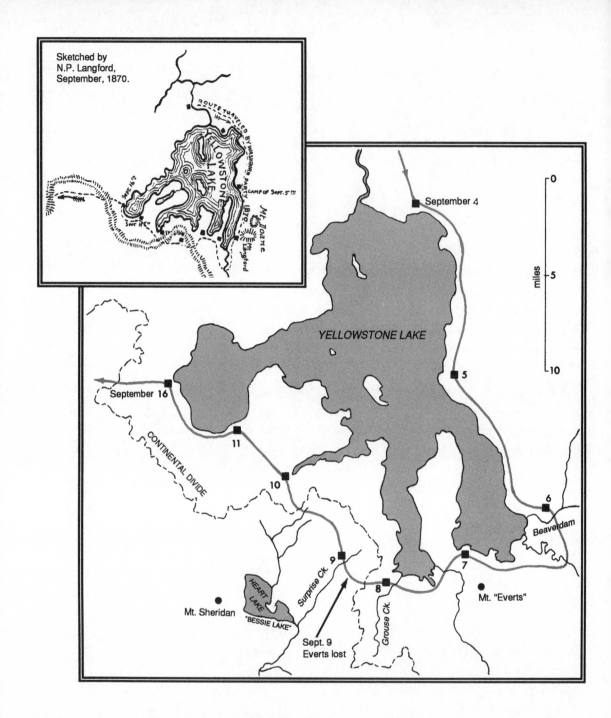

Sketched by
N.P. Langford,
September, 1870.

September 4

YELLOWSTONE LAKE

miles

0

5

10

September 16

5

CONTINENTAL DIVIDE

11

10

6

Beaverdam

Surprise Ck.

9

7

HEART LAKE

"BESSIE LAKE"

Mt. Sheridan

8

Grouse Ck.

Mt. "Everts"

Sept. 9
Everts lost

Map of Washburn expedition campsites showing where Everts was lost.

INTRODUCTION

Yellowstone's Most Famous Lost-in-the-Wilderness Story

Truman C. Everts's story of being lost for thirty-seven days in the wilderness of present Yellowstone National Park is an epic tale of survival. The story has been recounted a number of times by various authors,[1] but never so dramatically as in Everts's own account that was published in the November, 1871 issue of *Scribner's Monthly* magazine. That account, entitled "Thirty-Seven Days of Peril," is reprinted here in full. Everts was the first recorded person to become lost in the wilderness of present Yellowstone National Park. Others have been lost since him, but none for so long without dying. And none has ever recorded the experience in any comparable manner.

We know little about the actual writing of Everts's account. He wrote it after his adventure, and we do not know whether the editors of *Scribner's Monthly* polished it or otherwise changed it. Nor do we know how the original editors got the article, whose idea it was, or whether or not Everts was paid for it. Presumably he was. The Romantic prose style of the piece accords with contemporary writings and squares with Everts's few known other writings, largely letters.

1. Everts's account was reprinted in 1904 in *Contributions to the Historical Society of Montana* (vol. 5), in 1923 in a private booklet published in San Francisco by E. and R. Grabhorn and James McDonald, and in 1957 in *Montana Magazine of Western History* (7:29–52, October, 1957), but these versions were published without comments or much explanation. Secondary narratives of the Everts story are numerous, it having been told by A.L. Haines, H.M. Chittenden, Georgina Synge, James Richardson, and G.L. Henderson, among others. No full original account with comments and notes has been published until now.

Truman Everts (1816-1901), born at Burlington, Vermont, was one of six sons of a Great Lakes ship captain. He appears to have married at some time, and although nothing is known of that marriage, he did have a grown daughter named Elizabeth who kept house for him at Helena. He is known to have lived at various times in Michigan, Kentucky, New York, Montana, and finally Maryland.

P.W. Norris, later superintendent of Yellowstone, who traveled to the north boundary of the present park just prior to Everts's 1870 trip, met Everts during the Civil War at Fredericksburg, where Everts was serving as a Sanitary Commission Agent "kindly caring for the countless wounded." Norris and Everts became fast friends. Later, Norris wrote:

> Soon after [he was] appointed Assessor of Montana Territory he endured months of toilsome, dangerous travel via Salt Lake and Snake River Lava plain in reaching there. He continued a faithful, efficient officer and also trusty agent for my interests there until my arrival in Spring of 1870. We traveled together from Helena to Fort Ellis where he remained during my trip to Yellowstone, but we made the return trip and several others through various mountain passes together. When I started to descend the Columbia in August I left with him my original map and notes of the upper Yellowstone and they were lost with his own effects in the Park.[2]

2. P.W. Norris, "Meanderings of a Mountaineer, or, The Journals and Musings (or Storys) of a Rambler over Prairie (or Mountain) and Plain," letter 46, unpublished manuscript in Norris papers, Huntington Library, San Marino, California.

Everts was fifty-four when he became a member of the Washburn Expedition, a group of prominent Montana men who received essential

Truman C. Everts (1816–1901).

credit for the final discovery of what was to become Yellowstone National Park. That party was
the second phase of a three-stage effort—the Folsom party of 1869, the Washburn party of 1870,
and the Hayden party of 1871—that accomplished definitive exploration of today's park.
From the time of Lewis and Clark, the Yellowstone Plateau had been sketchily and often incredibly reported to contain volcanoes, boiling springs,
geysers, vents that could be ignited with a match,
glens deadly with poison gases, a huge crystal

lake, and waterfalls as tall as a thousand feet. Having heard those tales of strange wonders at the head of the Yellowstone River, these men determined to find out for themselves their veracity. The Washburn expedition was organized primarily to verify the fragmentary information they and others had heard from trappers, prospectors, and the Folsom party of the previous year. Although other parties predated it, the Washburn party has received most of the credit for "discovery" of the area, because it was the first to adequately report its findings. But so great were the wonders of the Yellowstone that it took several expeditions to make the world believe in them.

Five years before Everts's adventure, President Lincoln had appointed him Assessor of Internal Revenue for the new Territory of Montana. Losing that political position in early 1870, Everts stayed in the area hoping to find another job. But by midsummer, with nothing turning up, he had decided to return east with his grown daughter Elizabeth, or "Bessie," who as a belle of Helena society was being courted by another member of the 1870 Washburn party, Warren C. Gillette.

Everts's presence on the Washburn Expedition into the Yellowstone wilderness was therefore a kind of between-jobs vacation, although it turned into an experience that would sear his memory forever. He was the oldest member of the expedition, nearsighted but otherwise healthy, with no wilderness experience. The privations which befell him apparently did him no permanent harm, for in 1880 or 1881, when he was sixty-four or sixty-five, he was married to a fourteen-year-old.

The only known photograph of expedition members preparing to leave, probably packers Charles Reynolds and Elwyn Bean. This photograph, captioned "Packing a Recalcitrant Mule," appeared in Langford's 1905 book *Discovery of Yellowstone Park* with Langford's head on the man on the right.

Henry Dana Washburn (1832–1871), leader of the expedition, as he appeared in 1869.

Nathaniel Pitt Langford (1832–1909). The head from this photograph was reversed and used on the photo above in Langford's book, *Discovery of Yellowstone Park*.

Cornelius Hedges.

MEMBERS OF THE EXPEDITION.

Above left: Lt. Gustavus C. Doane (1840–1892).

Above right: Cornelius Hedges (1831–1907).

Right: Warren C. Gillette (1832–1912).

W. C. Gillette.

MEMBERS OF THE EXPEDITION.

Above left: Benjamin F. Stickney (1838–1912).

Above right: Samuel T. Hauser (1833–1914).

Left: Jacob W. Smith (1830–1897).

Above: Eastern shore of Heart Lake with Mount Sheridan in background— where Everts first saw Heart Lake. William Henry Jackson photo, 1878.

Right: Head of Yellowstone Lake, Southeast arm. The area where Everts was separated from his party. William Henry Jackson photo, 1871.

Above: Upper Falls of Yellowstone River and upper canyon. What Everts may have seen on the cold rainy day he returned to the canyon. William Henry Jackson photo, 1872.

Left: Everts thistle.

He fathered a son at nearly seventy-five and lived on another ten years after that. He spent his declining years at Hyattsville, Maryland, as a minor employee of the post office.[3]

The Washburn Expedition, consisting of nineteen men, forty horses, and a dog, entered the present park from the north, visiting Tower Fall, Mount Washburn, and the Upper and Lower Falls of the Yellowstone River. Traveling along the east shore of Yellowstone Lake, the party rounded the Southeast Arm on September 7 and camped on the shore of the lake, probably near one of the many unnamed creeks that flow into it south of the Molly Islands.

Here Everts and another party member, Cornelius Hedges, climbed the high plateau just south of the Southeast Arm of Yellowstone Lake, which today is the north end of Two Ocean Plateau. Hedges named this plateau "Mount Everts," a name that did not stick. Hedges's account of the climb appeared in the *Helena Daily Herald* for October 8, 1870, at a time when Everts was still lost in the wilderness.

The evening of the following day, September 8, 1870, the party camped on present Grouse Creek, east of Channel Mountain. On September 9, the party camped on the headwaters of Surprise Creek. Everts, having been split up from the main group during the day, did not come in. In a later letter to his sister, party member Cornelius Hedges stated that "the place where we lost him was in an almost impenetrable forest on the south shore of the Yellowstone Lake. We staid [sic] over a week looking for him or until we had barely enough provisions left to take us home."[4]

3. Aubrey L. Haines, *Yellowstone National Park: Its Exploration and Establishment* (Washington: GPO), 1974, pp. 139-40; *The Yellowstone Story* (Boulder: University of Colorado Press), I, pp. 106-36; Haines, audiotape interview with Truman C. Everts, Jr., Mammoth Hot Springs, Wyoming, August 11, 1961. Everts's son was born September 10, 1891.

4. Cornelius Hedges's letter to his sister, October 11, 1870, SC#1974, Montana Historical Society.

Other party members noted Everts's failure to arrive in camp. In his report, Lt. G.C. Doane stated, "Mr. Everts did not come in with the rest of the party, and the men sent back on the trail found no trace of him. We fired signal guns and kept watch fires during the night, but without success." Hedges noted in his journal, "All in but Everts and we felt well around the fire." A third party member, Warren Gillette, was concerned when the group camped at two o'clock:

> Here we learned to a certainty that Mr. Everts was lost. He was reported an hour or so before we stopped as not being with the train, but nothing was thought of it. Fired guns and halooed but could not get an answer. Some talk of not leaving this camp till he [is] found. Everts had matches which he took this morning, but has no Over Coat or blankets and no lariat for his horse. Has guns and ammunition [but] is near sighted.[5]

Thus began "Thirty-Seven Days of Peril" in the wilderness for fifty-four-year-old Truman C. Everts. During that time he kept alive mainly by subsisting on the roots of a thistle plant that has since been named the "Everts Thistle." The autumn Yellowstone weather was beginning to be intensely cold and wet, with winter snow already falling on some parts of the plateau. Everts, whose horse ran away taking most of his equipment, had almost nothing but the clothes on his back.

Here then is Truman C. Everts's own story.

5. G.C. Doane, "Report of Lieutenant Gustavus C. Doane Upon the So-called Yellowstone Expedition of 1870," 41st Cong., 3rd Sess, Sen. Ex. Doc. No. 51, 1873, p. 23; Cornelius Hedges, "Journal of Judge Cornelius Hedges," *Contributions to the Historical Society of Montana* 5 (1904):386; Brian Cockhill, "The Quest of Warren Gillette," *Montana Magazine of Western History* 22 (Summer, 1972):24. The Doane journal is published in Orrin and Lorraine Bonney's *Battle Drums and Geysers* (Chicago: Swallow Press, 1970).

Lost in the Yellowstone   Thirty-Seven Days
of Peril

I HAVE READ WITH great satisfaction the excellent descriptive articles on the wonders of the Upper Yellowstone, in the May and June numbers of your magazine.[1] Having myself been one of the party members who participated in many of the pleasures, and suffered all the perils of that expedition, I can not only bear testimony to the fidelity of the narrative, but probably add some facts of experience which will not detract from the general interest it thus excited.

A desire to visit this remarkable region, of which, during several years' residence in Montana, I had often heard the most marvelous accounts, led me to unite in the expedition of August last. The general character of the stupendous scenery of the Rocky Mountains prepared my mind for giving credit to all the strange stories told of the Yellowstone, and I felt quite as certain of the existence of the physical phenomena of that country, on the morning that our company started from Helena,[2] as when I afterwards beheld it. I engaged in the enterprise with enthusiasm, feeling that all the hardships and exposures of a month's horseback travel through an unexplored region

1. N.P. Langford, "The Wonders of the Yellowstone," *Scribner's Monthly* 2 (May, June), 1871.
2. August 17, 1870.

3

would be more than compensated by the grandeur and novelty of the natural objects with which it was crowded. Of course, the idea of being lost in it, without any of the ordinary means of subsistence, and of wandering for days and weeks, in a famishing condition, alone, in an unfrequented wilderness, formed no part of my contemplation. I had dwelt too long amid the mountains not to know that such a thought, had it occurred, would have been instantly rejected as improbable; nevertheless, "man proposes and God disposes," a truism which found a new and ample illustration in my wanderings through the Upper Yellowstone region.

My friend Langford has so well described the scenery and physical eccentricities of the country, that I should feel that any attempt to amplify it would be to

"Guild refined gold and paint the lily."

My narrative must, therefore, be strictly personal.

On the day that I found myself separated from the company,[3] and for several days previous, our course had been impeded by the dense growth of the pine forest, and occasional large tracts of fallen timber, frequently rendering our progress almost impossible. Whenever we came to one of these immense windfalls, each man engaged in the pursuit of a passage through it, and it was while thus employed, and with the idea that I had found one, that I strayed out of sight and hearing of my comrades. We had a toilsome day. It was quite late in the afternoon. As separations like this had frequently occurred,[4] it gave me no alarm, and I

3. September 9, 1870. The night before this, the Washburn party had camped on Grouse Creek (see map). On the ninth, they were in the process of moving to their next camp on the headwaters of Surprise Creek. Everts did not come into camp that evening.

4. Everts had been previously separated from the party at Bottler's ranch when he became sick from eating too many wild berries, but he caught up to the party with no trouble. And Cornelius Hedges was to note later in a letter to his sister that he, too, had become separated at several points from the party: "I was often seperated [sic] from the train but never had any difficulty in finding my way back." Hedges to sister, October 11, 1870, Montana Historical Society, SC #1974.

rode on, fully confident of soon rejoining the company, or of finding their camp. I came up with the pack-horse, which Mr. Langford afterwards recovered, and tried to drive him along, but failing to do so, and my eyesight being defective, I spurred forward, intending to return with assistance from the party. This incident tended to accelerate my speed. I rode on in the direction which I supposed had been taken, until darkness overtook me in the dense forest. This was disagreeable enough, but caused me no alarm. I had no doubt of being with the party at breakfast the next morning. I selected a spot for comfortable repose, picketed my horse, built a fire, and went to sleep.

The next morning[5] I rose at early dawn, saddled and mounted my horse, and took my course in the supposed direction of the camp. Our ride of the previous day had been up a peninsula jutting into the lake, for the shore of which I started, with the expectation of finding my friends camped on the beach. The forest was quite dark, and the trees so thick, that it was only by a slow process I could get through them at all.[6] In searching for the trail I became somewhat confused. The falling foliage of the pines had obliterated every trace of travel. I was obliged frequently to dismount, and examine the ground for the faintest indications. Coming to an opening, from which I could see several vistas, I dismounted for the purpose of selecting one leading in the direction I had chosen, and leaving my horse unhitched, as had always been my custom, walked a few rods into the forest. While surveying the

5. This was September 10. The rest of the party was heading northwest toward a camp on Flat Mountain Arm where they would build a large signal fire high above the lake and fire off their guns to signal Everts. Upon their arrival in camp, Gillette and Trumbull backtracked along the lakeshore to look for Everts and even spent the night out searching for him. N.P. Langford, *The Discovery of Yellowstone Park* (Lincoln: University of Nebraska Press, 1972), p. 77.

6. The peninsula Everts is discussing here is probably the large body of land between the South Arm and Thumb Bay. Aubrey L. Haines to Tom Tankersley, October 17, 1994.

Hedges wrote of their experiences near here: "The southern shore is an almost impenetrable timbered wilderness, through which we toiled and swore our way, coming out after several days tattered and torn, ragged, bleeding, and sullen. We had lost one of our company and only wondered that we had not lost all of them. Future generations may find on this south shore hallowed grounds, but it was soundly and sorely cursed by us." Hedges, "Yellowstone Lake," Helena *Daily Herald*, November 9, 1870.

"THE LAST I EVER SAW OF HIM"

7. A newspaper article published after Everts was found stated that Everts's horse ran away with everything "except a butcher-knife, which he had on his person." Helena *Daily Herald*, October 26, 1870. Everts's friend P.W. Norris later lamented the loss of Norris's own map and notes, saying, "his gun, equipments, and entire outfit, including my map, notes, etc., left with him, were totally lost, and no trace of them ever has been, or perhaps ever will be found." P.W. Norris, "Meanderings of a Mountaineer, or, The Journals and Musings (or Storys) of a Rambler over Prairie (or Mountain) and Plain," letter #4, August 16, 1870, unpublished manuscript in Norris papers, Huntington Library, San Marino, California.

Many secondhand mentions of Everts's adventure include the claim that he "lost" his glasses, one account apparently getting this information from another without further investigation. Unless we count Everts's apparent *breaking* of his "spectacles," I have been unable to confirm that this ever happened. It is not mentioned in Everts's own account, nor in any other firsthand accounts that I have found. I suspect the reason for the story stems at least partly from the fact that Lt. G.C. Doane reported that Everts was very nearsighted. Another possibility for the story may be confusion with Everts's opera glass which he used to make fires, for he did lose it at one point and backtracked to find it. Regardless, it appears that Everts never "lost" his glasses. In fact, later we note that he tried to make a fishhook "from the rim of my broken spectacles."

8. None of Everts's written notices were found by other party members. They too left notices. Langford stated on September 11, "On leaving our camps yesterday and today, we posted conspicuously at each a placard, stating clearly the direction we had taken and where provisions could be found." Langford, *Discovery*, p. 80.

ground my horse took fright, and I turned around in time to see him disappearing at full speed among the trees. That was the last I ever saw of him. It was yet quite dark. My blankets, gun, pistols, fishing tackle, matches—everything, except the clothing on my person, a couple of knives, and a small opera-glass were attached to the saddle.[7]

I did not yet realize the possibility of a permanent separation from the company. Instead of following up the pursuit of their camp, I engaged in an effort to recover my horse. Half a day's search convinced me of its impracticability. I wrote and posted in an open space several notices,[8] which, if my friends should chance to see, would inform them of my condition and the route I had taken, and then struck out into the forest in the supposed direction of their camp. As the day wore on without any discovery, alarm took the place of anxiety at the prospect of another night alone in the wilderness, and this time without food or fire. But even this dismal foreboding was cheered by the hope that I should soon rejoin my companions, who would laugh at my adventure, and incorporate it as a thrilling episode into the journal of our trip. The bright side of a misfortune, as I found by experience, even under the worst possible circumstances, always presents some features of encouragement. When I began to realize that my condition was one of actual peril, I banished from my mind all fear of an unfavorable result. Seating myself on a log, I recalled every foot of the way I had travelled since the separation from my friends, and the most probable opinion I could form of their whereabouts was, that they had, by a course but little different from mine, passed by the spot where I had posted the notices, learned of my disaster, and were waiting for me to rejoin them there, or searching for me in that vicinity. A night must be spent amid the prostrate trunks before my return could be accomplished. At no time during my period of exile did I experience so much mental suffering from the cravings of hunger as when, exhausted with this long day of fruitless search, I resigned myself to a couch of pine foliage in the pitchy darkness of a thicket of small trees. Naturally timid in the night, I fully realized the exposure of my condition. I peered upward through the darkness, but all was blackness and

9. Everts's recognition of the sound of the wolf, as distinguished from that of the coyote, is one more proof of the wolf's early presence in the Yellowstone country. It is not surprising that a person alone, as opposed to a larger group, would see and hear more animals. For a historical analysis of wolves and other animals in Yellowstone in early days that discusses Everts's sighting of animals, see Paul Schullery and Lee Whittlesey, "Documentary Record of Wolves and Related Wildlife Species in the Yellowstone National Park Area Prior to 1882," in *Wolves for Yellowstone?*, vol. IV (Yellowstone Research Division, 1992).

At this same time (September 10) the rest of the party had moved camp to the head of the Flat Mountain Arm. They climbed the mountain, lighted a beacon fire, and fired signal guns during the night, but to no avail.

10. September 11, 1870. The lodgepole pine (*Pinus contorta*) covers about eighty percent of the park. In areas where no forest fires have burned for many years, deadfall like many jackstraws impedes one's path.

The rest of Everts's party used this day to search for him up and down the beach of Yellowstone Lake. Langford, *Discovery*, p. 79. Gillette and Trumbull, who had spent the night out looking for Everts, returned to this camp, which was located four miles from West Thumb. Gillette says he left notes for Everts in two different places along the lakeshore. The party decided to remain here several days to look for Everts.

11. Everts was hoping to beat (or meet) the main party to/at the west shore of the lake, the present West Thumb area, as the group had previously planned. Langford has stated that before Everts was lost, the party had a discussion as to what they would all do if someone were to become lost:

and we agreed that in such case we would all move on as rapidly as possible to the southwest arm of the lake, where there are hot springs . . . and there remain until all the party were united. Everts thought a better way for a lost man would be to strike out nearly due west, hoping to

gloom. The wind sighed mournfully through the pines. The forest seemed alive with the screeching of night birds, the angry barking of coyotes, and the prolonged, dismal howl of the gray wolf.[9] These sounds, familiar by their constant occurrence throughout the journey, were now full of terror, and drove slumber from my eye-lids. Above all this, however, was the hope that I should be restored to my comrades the next day.

Early the next morning I rose unrefreshed, and pursued my weary way over the prostrate trunks.[10] It was noon when I reached the spot where my notices were posted. No one had been there. My disappointment was almost overwhelming. For the first time, I realized that I was lost. Then came a crushing sense of destitution. No food, no fire; no means to procure either; alone in an unexplored wilderness, one hundred and fifty miles from the nearest human abode, surrounded by wild beasts, and famishing with hunger. It was no time for despondency. A moment afterwards I felt how calamity can elevate the mind, in the formation of the resolution "not to perish in that wilderness."

The hope of finding the party still controlled my plans. I thought, by traversing the peninsula centrally, I would be enabled to strike the shore of the lake in advance of their camp, and near the point of departure for the Madison.[11] Acting upon this impression, I rose from a sleepless couch, and pursued my way through the timber-entangled forest. A feeling of weakness took the place of hunger. Conscious of the need of food, I felt no cravings. Occasionally, while scrambling over logs and through thickets, a sense of faintness and exhaustion would come over me, but I would suppress it with the audible expression, "This won't do; I *must* find my company." Despondency would sometimes strive with resolution for the mastery of my thoughts. I would think of home—of my daughter[12]—and of the possible chance of starvation, or death in some more terrible form; but as often as these gloomy forebodings came, I would strive to banish them with reflections better adapted to my immediate necessities. I recollect at this time discussing the question, whether there was not implanted by Providence in every man a principle of self-preservation equal to any emergency which did not destroy his reason. I decided this question affirmatively a thousand times afterwards in my wanderings, and I record this experience here, that any person who reads it, should he ever find himself in like circumstances, may not despair. There is life in the thought. It will revive hope, allay hunger, renew energy, encourage perseverance, and, as I have proved in my own case, bring a man out of difficulty, when nothing else can avail.

It was mid-day when I emerged from the forest into an open space at the foot of the peninsula. A broad lake of beautiful curvature, with magnificent surroundings, lay before me, glittering in the sunbeams. It was full twelve miles in circumference.[13] A wide belt of sand formed the margin which I was approaching, directly opposite to which, rising seemingly from the very depths of the water, towered the loftiest peak of a range of mountains apparently interminable.[14] The ascending vapor from innumerable hot springs, and

reach the headwaters of the Madison river, and follow that stream as his guide to the settlements; but he finally abandoned this idea and adopted that which has been approved by the rest of the party.
Langford, *Discovery*, p. 77.
Moreover, according to Langford, Everts had even emphasized this solution to Hedges: "On the evening that Mr. Hedges was lost, Mr. Everts told him that he ought to have struck out for the [Yellowstone] lake, as he (Everts) would do if lost." Langford, *Discovery*, p. 79. So it is difficult to understand why Everts did not immediately strike out for Yellowstone Lake where he would have found his friends.

12. Elizabeth "Bessie" Everts of Helena, who sometimes dated Warren Gillette of the party.

13. Heart Lake. Everts was on its eastern shore. It was midday of September 11, 1870. His comrades at this time were deciding to remain for three more days in their camp on Flat Mountain Arm, preparing to continue searching for him. Langford, *Discovery*, pp. 79-80. It is not known why Everts went to Heart Lake instead of heading for West Thumb as his party had agreed to do if anyone were lost. Perhaps he simply got turned around and went the wrong direction. At any rate, arguably he should have realized at this point that he was not on Yellowstone Lake and should have used the rest of the day to hunt for West Thumb. He could have climbed nearby Mount Sheridan to determine which way to travel if he was confused. Instead Everts remained at Heart Lake, out of the reach of party members.

14. Mount Sheridan and the Red Mountain Range.

15. Everts was looking across the lake at the Rustic Group of hot springs of Heart Lake Geyser Basin. The geyser he saw was probably present Rustic Geyser.

16. Yellowstone Park bird specialist Terry McEneaney believes that this bird was a Townsend's solitaire, which sounds much like a mockingbird. Everts's account of seeing all of this wildlife at Heart Lake is corroborated by Doane's account of Privates Williamson and Moore, who also found wildlife abundant near Heart Lake. Schullery and Whittlesey, "Documentary Record . . . ," pp. 1–57.

17. Everts was not correct. The lake had been seen in 1839 by fur trapper Osborne Russell (see Aubrey L. Haines, ed., *Journal of a Trapper* (Lincoln: University of Nebraska Press, 1965), p. 106 &n165). Arnold Hague, eminent Yellowstone geologist, believed that John Colter saw Heart Lake on his winter trip of 1807–08, but this cannot be strictly verified. National Archives, Record Group 57, Arnold Hague papers, box 10, unpublished notes for Monograph 32, pt. 1, chapter 3, p. 10.

18. Everts is esssentially correct here.

19. Everts is wrong here. The peak today is called Mount Sheridan. Cornelius Hedges had given the name "Mount Everts" to the north end of present Two Ocean Plateau. And General H.D. Washburn had earlier named present Colter Peak "Mount Langford." Possibly Everts got the two locations confused. Because of Everts's experiences at its base, present Mount Sheridan is arguably the peak that should have the name Everts.

the sparkling jet of a single geyser, added the feature of novelty to one of the grandest landscapes I ever beheld.[15] Nor was the life of the scene less noticeable than its other attractions. Large flocks of swans and other water-fowl were sporting on the quiet surface of the lake; otters in great numbers performed the most amusing aquatic evolutions; mink and beaver swam around unscared, in most grotesque confusion. Deer, elk, and mountain sheep stared at me, manifesting more surprise than fear at my presence among them. The adjacent forest was vocal with the songs of birds, chief of which were the chattering notes of a species of mockingbird, whose imitative efforts afforded abundant merriment.[16] Seen under favorable circumstances, this assemblage of grandeur, beauty, and novelty would have been transporting; but, jaded with travel, famishing with hunger, and distressed with anxiety, I was in no humor for ecstasy. My tastes were subdued and chastened by the perils which environed me. I longed for food, friends, and protection. Associated with my thoughts, however, was the wish that some of my friends of peculiar tastes could enjoy this display of secluded magnificence, now, probably, for the first time beheld by mortal eyes.[17]

The lake was at least one thousand feet lower than the highest point of the peninsula, and several hundred feet below the level of Yellowstone Lake.[18] I recognized the mountain which overshadowed it as the landmark which, a few days before, had received from Gen. Washburn the name of Mount Everts;[19] and as it is associated with some of the most agreeable and terrible incidents of my exile, I feel that I have more than a mere discoverer's right to the perpetuity of that christening. The lake is fed by innumerable small streams from the mountains, and the countless hot springs surrounding it. A large river[20] flows from it, through a cañon a thousand feet in height, in a southeasterly direction, to a distant range of mountains, which I conjectured to be Snake River; and with the belief that I had discovered the source of the great southern tributary of the Columbia, I gave it the name of Bessie Lake, after the

"Sole daughter of my house and heart."

During the first two days, the fear of meeting with Indians gave me considerable anxiety;[21] but, when conscious of being lost, there was nothing I so much desired as to fall in with a lodge of Bannacks [sic] or Crows. Having nothing to tempt their cupidity, they would do me no personal harm, and, with the promise of reward, would probably minister to my wants and aid my deliverance. Imagine my delight, while gazing upon the animated expanse of water, at seeing sail out from a distant point a large canoe containing a single oarsman. It was rapidly approaching the shore where I was seated. With hurried steps I paced the beach to meet it, all my energies stimulated by the assurance it gave of food, safety, and restoration to friends. As I drew near to it it turned towards the shore, and oh! bitter disappointment, the object which my eager fancy had transformed into an angel of relief stalked from the water, an enormous pelican, flapped its dragon-wings as if in mockery of my sorrow, and flew to a solitary point farther up the lake. This

20. Heart River, which flows south into Snake River. The true head of Snake River was determined two years later to be a distance southeast of Heart Lake near the Continental Divide.

21. Apparently, Everts was worrying about the Indians the party had encountered during the early days of their trip near the present north boundary of the park.

little incident quite unmanned me. The transition from joy to grief brought with it a terrible consciousness of the horrors of my condition. But night was fast approaching, and darkness would come with it. While looking for a spot where I might repose in safety, my attention was attracted to a small green plant of so lively a hue as to form a striking contrast with the deep pine foliage. For closer examination I pulled it up by the root, which was long and tapering, not unlike a radish. It was a thistle. I tasted it; it was palatable and nutritious. My appetite craved it, and the first meal in four days was made on thistle-roots. Eureka! I had found food. No optical illusion deceived me this time; I could subsist until I rejoined my companions. Glorious counterpoise to the wretchedness of the preceding half-hour![22]

Overjoyed at this discovery, with hunger allayed, I stretched myself under a tree, upon the foliage which had partially filled a space between contiguous trunks, and fell asleep. How long I slept I know not; but suddenly I was roused by a loud, shrill scream, like that of a human being in distress, poured, seemingly, into the very portals of my ear. There was no mistaking that fearful voice. I had been deceived by and answered it a dozen times while threading the forest, with the belief that it was a friendly signal. It was the screech of a mountain lion, so alarmingly near as to cause every nerve to thrill with terror. To yell in return, seize with convulsive grasp the limbs of the friendly tree, and swing myself into it, was the work of a moment. Scrambling hurriedly from limb to limb, I was soon as near the top as safety

22. The elk thistle (*Cirsium foliosum*) has since been renamed Everts Thistle. Everts's friend P.W. Norris wrote of it: "The thistle so prominent in his [Everts's] narrative is peculiar to those volcanic regions. From knee to belt high it is very stocky, branched and prickly with many heads in blossom at once, altogether a pestiferous plant save the large tap root upon which Indians, as Everts did, for a time subsist." Norris, "Meanderings . . . ," Note *A* in letter 46.

THE MOUNTAIN LION

would permit. The savage beast was snuffing and growling below, apparently on the very spot I had just abandoned. I answered every growl with a responsive scream. Terrified at the delay and pawing of the beast, I increased my voice to its utmost volume, broke branches from the limbs, and, in the impotency of fright, madly hurled them at the spot whence the continued howlings proceeded.

Failing to alarm the animal, which now began to make the circuit of the tree, as if to select a spot for springing into it, I shook, with a strength increased by terror, the slender trunk until every limb rustled with the motion. All in vain. The terrible creature pursued his walk around the tree, lashing the ground with his tail, and prolonging his howlings almost to a roar. It was too dark to see, but the movements of the lion kept me apprised of its position. Whenever I heard it on one side of the tree I speedily changed to the opposite—an exercise which, in my weakened state, I could only have performed under the impulse of terror. I would alternately sweat and thrill with horror at the thought of being torn to pieces and devoured by this formidable monster. All my attempts to frighten it seemed unavailing. Disheartened at its persistency, and expecting every moment it would take the deadly leap, I tried to collect my thoughts, and prepare for the fatal encounter which I knew must result. Just at this moment it occurred to me that I would try silence. Clasping the trunk of the tree with both arms, I sat perfectly still. The lion, at this time ranging round, occasionally snuffing and pausing, and all the while filling the forest with the echo of his howlings, suddenly imitated my example. This silence was more terrible, if possible, than the clatter and crash of his movements through the brushwood, for now I did not know from what direction to expect his attack. Moments passed with me like hours. After a lapse of time which I cannot estimate, the beast gave a spring into the thicket and ran screaming into the forest. My deliverance was effected.[23]

Had strength permitted, I should have retained my perch till daylight, but with the consciousness of escape from the jaws of the ferocious brute came a sense of overpowering weakness which almost palsied me, and made my descent from the

23. The mountain lion (*Felis concolor*) is now nearly extinct in Yellowstone Park. But there are far too many reports by early visitors of sightings of this animal or of the hearings of its screams for one not to conclude that more lions lived in Yellowstone in the 1870s than do now. Schullery and Whittlesey, "Documentary Record . . . ," pp. 1–150. Yellowstone Park lion researcher Kerry Murphy says that in 1994, only 25–35 lions are known to inhabit the Park. Apparently, a mountain lion tracked Everts during his last days of being lost, only to be killed by Jack Baronett.

Interestingly, Everts's friends also heard this or another mountain lion at about the same time while camped at West Thumb. Langford says, " . . . our ears were saluted with a shriek so terribly human, that for a moment we believed it to be a call from Mr. Everts, and we hallooed in response, and several of our party started in the direction whence the sounds came, and would have instituted a search for our comrade but for an admonitory growl of a mountain lion." Langford, *Discovery*, p. 80.

tree both difficult and dangerous. Incredible as it may seem, I lay down in my old bed, and was soon lost in a slumber so profound that I did not awake until after daylight.[24] The experience of the night seemed like a terrible dream; but the broken limbs which in the agony of consternation I had thrown from the tree, and the rifts made in the fallen foliage by my visitant in his circumambulations, were too convincing evidence of its reality. I could not dwell upon my exposure and escape without shuddering, and reflecting that probably like perils would often occur under less fortunate circumstances, and with a more fatal issue. I wondered what fate was in reserve for me— whether I would ultimately sink from exhaustion and perish of starvation, or become the prey of some of the ferocious animals that roamed these vast fastnesses. My thoughts then turned to the loved ones at home. They could never know my fate, and would indulge a thousand conjectures concerning it, not the least distressing of which would be that I had been captured by a band of hostile Sioux, and tortured to death at the stake.

I was roused from this train of reflections by a marked change in the atmosphere. One of those dreary storms of mingled snow and rain, common to these high latitudes, set in. My clothing, which had been much torn, exposed my person to its "pitiless peltings." An easterly wind, rising to a gale, admonished me that it would be furious and of long duration. None of the discouragements I had met with dissipated the hope of rejoining my friends; but foreseeing the delay, now unavoidable, I knew that my escape from the wilderness

24. If Everts's chronology is correct, this was the morning of September 12, 1870. But probably it is not correct and it is really the thirteenth, for Langford states that it began to rain and hail at 9 A.M. on the thirteenth, probably the "dreary storm" that Everts soon comments on. Langford, *Discovery*, p. 89. On the twelfth, Everts's friends began a search for him, sending out three parties in different directions to search for him: Smith and Trumbull along the lakeshore to their last camp, Hauser and Gillette back on their trail through the woods, and Washburn and Langford riding south to the north end of Heart Lake, where Langford's horse broke through thin crust in a thermal area. Hedges remained in camp in case Everts showed up.

Again they left notices, as Langford stated, "At all of our camps for the past three days, and along the line of travel between them, we have blazed the trees as a guide for Mr. Everts, and have left a small supply of provisions at each place, securely cached, with notices directing Mr. Everts to the places of concealment." Langford, *Discovery*, p. 83.

must be accomplished, if at all, by my own unaided exertions. This thought was terribly afflicting, and brought before me, in vivid array, all the dreadful realities of my condition. I could see no ray of hope. In this condition of mind I could find no better shelter than the spreading branches of a spruce tree, under which, covered with earth and boughs, I lay during the two succeeding days; the storm, meanwhile, raging with unabated violence. While thus exposed, and suffering from cold and hunger, a little benumbed bird, not larger than a snow-bird, hopped within my reach. I instantly seized and killed it, and, plucking its feathers, ate it raw. It was a delicious meal for a half-starved man.

Taking advantage of a lull in the elements on the morning of the third day I rose early and started in the direction of a large group of hot springs which were steaming under the shadow of Mount Everts. The distance I traveled could not have been less than ten miles.[25] Long before I reached the wonderful cluster of natural caldrons, the storm had recommenced. Chilled through, with my clothing thoroughly saturated, I lay down under a tree upon the heated incrustation until completely warmed. My heels and the sides of my feet were frozen. As soon as warmth had permeated my system, and I had quieted my appetite with a few thistle-roots, I took a survey of my surroundings, and selected a spot between two springs sufficiently asunder to afford heat at my head and feet.[26] On this spot I built a bower of pine branches, spread its incrusted surface with fallen foliage and small boughs, and stowed myself away to await the close of the storm. Thistles

25. It only seemed like ten miles around the sandy beach of Heart Lake. Actually the distance around the lake to Rustic Geyser from the mouth of Beaver Creek is three to four miles. Everts had broken onto the shore of the lake somewhere on its eastern side, probably onto the peninsula that juts into the lake from the north. If Everts's chronology is correct, it was September 13, 1870, the morning of his fourth full day lost. But as mentioned earlier, Everts's chronology is probably confused and this could be September 14. His friends (again) remained in camp all that day at West Thumb because the snow was two feet deep. Gillette lamented, "Poor Everts I fear he has perished." Gillette in Brian Cockhill, "The Quest of Warren Gillette," *Montana Magazine of Western History* 22 (Summer, 1972):25.

26. The exact two springs he slept between are of course not known. Dr. A.C. Peale's map of 1878 showed twenty-nine hot springs in the Rustic Group at Heart Lake.

were abundant, and I had fed upon them long enough to realize that they would, for a while at least, sustain life. In convenient proximity to my abode was a small, round, boiling spring, which I called my dinner-pot, and in which, from time to time, I cooked my roots.

This establishment, the best I could improvise with the means at hand, I occupied seven days[27]—the first three of which were darkened by one of the most furious storms I ever saw. The vapor which supplied me with warmth saturated my clothing with its condensations. I was enveloped in a perpetual steam-bath. At first this was barely preferable to the storm, but I soon became accustomed to it, and before I left, though thoroughly parboiled, actually enjoyed it.

I had little else to do during my imprisonment but cook, think, and sleep. Of the variety and strangeness of my reflections it is impossible to give the faintest conception. Much of my time was given to devising means for escape. I recollected to have read, at the time of their publication, the narratives of Lieutenant Strain and Doctor Kane, and derived courage and hope from the reflection that they struggled with and survived perils not unlike those which environed me. The chilling thought would then occur, that they were not alone. They had companions in suffering and sympathy. Each could bear his share of the burden of misery which it fell to my lot to bear alone, and make it lighter from the encouragement of mutual counsel and aid in a cause of common suffering. Selfish as the thought may seem, there was nothing I so much desired as a companion in

27. According to this statement, Everts stayed here at the foot of Mount Sheridan September 12–18, 1870, finally leaving on the morning of the nineteenth, but he had apparently arrived there midday of the eleventh. Langford and Washburn rode south on September 12 toward Heart Lake during Everts's stay at the hot springs and were within a mile of the lake's north shore when Langford's horse broke through a thin hot spring turf, probably in the present Fissure Springs Group of Heart Lake Geyser Basin. Thus they abandoned their search. Had they pressed on to the lake, they would have found the unhappy Everts.

On the fifteenth, the party again remained in camp, but the weather moderated when rain and sunshine melted the snow. Langford, *Scribner's Monthly*, June, 1871, p. 120. Langford wondered how Everts was faring in the snow. *Discovery*, p. 93. Gillette stated,

This snow is a sad thing for Everts. How I pity him, hungry, wet and cold. I wonder if he killed his mare. I would do it and dry the meat, so I could pack enough on my back to carry me to the settlements. It is all conjecture as to the way he went. Some [of the party] think by Snake River, some back, others and nearly all, myself included, think he has turned to the Madison and made for Virginia City. I fear he is still wandering in the Mountains bewildered. It seems useless to search, but more effort must be made.

Gillette in Cockhill, p. 26.

On the sixteenth, the party moved around the lakeshore, five miles per Gillette, to a camp at present West Thumb Geyser Basin. On the seventeenth they left Gillette and two others to search for Everts and the rest headed west toward Old Faithful.

misfortune. How greatly it would alleviate my distress! What a relief it would be to compare my wretchedness with that of a brother sufferer, and with him devise expedients for every exigency as it occurred! I confess to the weakness, if it be one, of having squandered much pity upon myself during the time I had little else to do.

Nothing gave me more concern than the want of fire. I recalled everything I had ever read or heard of the means by which fire could be produced; but none of them were within my reach. An escape without it was simply impossible. It was indispensable as a protection against night attacks from wild beasts. Exposure to another storm like the one just over would destroy my life, as this one would have done, but for the warmth derived from the springs. As I lay in my bower anxiously awaiting the disappearance of the snow, which had fallen to the depth of a foot or more, and impressed with the belief that for want of fire I should be obliged to remain among the springs, it occurred to me that I would erect some sort of monument, which might, at some future day, inform a casual visitor of the circumstances under which I had perished. A gleam of sunshine lit up the bosom of the lake, and with it the thought flashed upon my mind that I could, with a lens from my opera-glasses, get fire from Heaven. Oh, happy, life-renewing thought! Instantly subjecting it to the test of experiment, when I saw the smoke curl from the bit of dry wood in my fingers, I felt, if the whole world were offered me for it, I would cast it all aside before parting with that little spark. I was now the happy possessor of food and fire. These would carry me through. All thoughts of failure were instantly abandoned. Though the food was barely adequate to my necessities—a fact too painfully attested by my attenuated body—I had forgotten the cravings of hunger, and had the means of producing fire. I said to myself, "I will not despair."

My stay at the springs was prolonged several days by an accident that befell me on the third night after my arrival there. An unlucky movement while asleep broke the crust on which I reposed, and the hot steam, pouring upon my hip, scalded it severely before I could escape. This new affliction, added to my frost-bitten feet, already festering, was the cause of frequent delay and unceasing pain through all my wanderings. After obtaining fire, I set to work making preparations for as early departure as my condition would permit. I had lost both knives since parting from the company, but I now made a convenient substitute by sharpening the tongue of a buckle which I cut from my vest. With this I cut the legs and counters from my boots, making of them a passable pair of slippers, which I fastened to my feet as firmly as I could with strips of bark. With the ravelings of a linen handkerchief, aided by the magic buckle-tongue, I mended my clothing. Of the same material I made a fish-line, which, on finding a piece of red tape in one of my pockets better suited to the purpose, I abandoned as a "bad job." I made of a pin that I found in my coat a fish-hook, and, by sewing up the bottoms of my boot-legs, constructed a very good pair of pouches to carry my food in, fastening them to my belt by the straps.[28]

Thus accoutered, on the morning of the eighth day after my arrival at the springs I bade them a

28. In a later interview, Everts told Samuel Langhorne that the fishhook was made of the breeches buckle and the fishline was made of pieces of canvas. Helena *Daily Herald*, October 26, 1870.

29. If Everts is correct in his chronology, it was September 19 (or less likely September 20), 1870. Everts means the southwest arm of Yellowstone Lake, or the present West Thumb area, where he expected to find his friends. During his delay in getting there, they had gone on. Gillette was especially concerned about the loss of Everts, because there was a possibility that Everts would become his future father-in-law. Washburn wrote, "Mr. Gillette volunteered to stay and prolong the search, and two soldiers were left with him. Mr. Gillette is one of the best mountain men of the party, and there is hope that he may bring some tidings of the missing man." H.D. Washburn, "The Yellowstone Expedition," 42nd Cong., 1st Sess., House Ex. Doc. No. 10, SN-1470, March 21, 1871, p. 215.

On the morning of the seventeenth, Langford and the others were disconsolate:

This has been a gloomy morning in our camp, for we all have been depressed at the thought of leaving the lake and abandoning the search for Mr. Everts. We have discussed the situation from every point of view, and have tried to put ourselves in his place and have considered all the possibilities of fate that may befall him. At one moment he may be buoyed up with hope, however faint—at another weighed down by despair and fear, with all their mental terrors. Has he met death by accident, or may he be injured and unable to move, and be suffering the horrors of starvation and fever? Has he wandered aimlessly hither and thither until bereft of reason? As I contemplate all these possibilities, it is a relief to think that he may have lost his life at the hand of some vagabond Indian.

Langford, *Discovery*, pp. 99–100.

30. The main party's conjectures about Everts's disappearance have been summed up by N.P. Langford:

Search was made for him for 7 days— each one of our party who had any reasonable hope of finding his own way back to camp, joining in its prosecution; and I assure you that this was no trifling mat-

final farewell, and started on my course directly across that portion of the neck of the peninsula between me and the southeast arm of Yellowstone Lake.[29] It was a beautiful morning. The sun shone bright and warm, and there was a freshness in the atmosphere truly exhilarating. As I wandered musingly along, the consciousness of being alone, and of having surrendered all hope of finding my friends, returned upon me with crushing power. I felt, too, that those friends, by the necessities of their condition, had been compelled to abandon all efforts for my recovery[.] The thought was full of bitterness and sorrow. I tried to realize what their conjectures were concerning my disappearance;[30] but could derive no consolation from the long and dismal train of circumstances they suggested. Weakened by a long fast, and the unsatisfying nature of the only food I could procure, I know that from this time onward to the day of my rescue, my mind, though unimpaired in those perceptions needful to self-preservation, was in a condition to receive impressions akin to insanity. I was constantly traveling in dream-land, and indulging in strange reveries such as I had never known before. I seemed to possess a sort of duality of being, which, while constantly reminding me of the necessities of my condition, fed my imagination with vagaries of the most extravagant character. Nevertheless, I was perfectly conscious of the tendency of these morbid influences, and often tried to shake them off, but they would ever return with increased force, and I finally reasoned myself into the belief that their indulgence, as it afforded me pleasure,

THE FIRST FIRE

could work no harm while it did not interfere with my plans for deliverance. Thus I lived in a world of ideal happiness, and in a world of positive suffering at the same time.

A change in the wind and an overcast sky, accompanied by cold, brought with them a need of warmth. I drew out my lens and touchwood, but alas! there was no sun. I sat down on a log to await his friendly appearance. Hours passed; he did not come. Night, cold, freezing night, set in, and found me exposed to all its terrors. A bleak hillside sparsely covered with pines afforded poor accommodations for a half-clad, famishing man. I

ter, for two of our best trailsmen who returned 4 days march would have been utterly lost but for the sagacity of their dog, which led them by his keen scent through the deep snow that had fallen, to camp. At every point that it was conceived that our comrade might pass, in his search for the lake shore, we made a cache of provisions and matches, protected by rocks and boulders from wild beasts, and conspicuously posted notices of this fact, on the trees near by. After seven days unavailing search, we concluded that Mr. Everts had been shot from his horse by some straggling indian, or had followed down a tributary of Snake River on which we camped the day he was lost, and had reached some settlement—and leaving three of our party with nearly all our provisions to still prosecute the search, we returned home . . . .

N.P. Langford, handwritten "Mss. of Lectures Given by N.P. Langford during winter of 1870–71," original at YNP Library, pp. 119–21.

could only keep from freezing by the most active exertion in walking, rubbing and striking my benumbed feet and hands against the logs. It seemed the longest, most terrible night of my life, and glad was I when the approaching dawn enabled me to commence retracing my steps to Bessie Lake. I arrived there at noon, built my first fire on the beach, and remained by it, recuperating, for the succeeding two days.[31]

The faint hope that my friends might be delayed by their search for me until I could rejoin them now forsook me altogether. I made my arrangements independent of it. Either of three directions I might take would effect my escape, if life and strength held out. I drew upon the sand of the beach a map of these several courses with reference to my starting-point from the lake, and considered well the difficulties each would present. All were sufficiently defined to avoid mistake. One was to follow Snake River a distance of one hundred miles or more to Eagle Rock bridge; another, to cross the country between the southern shore of Yellowstone Lake and the Madison Mountains, by scaling which I could easily reach the settlements in the Madison Valley; and the other, to retrace my journey over the long and discouraging route by which I had entered the country. Of these routes the last-mentioned seemed the least inviting, probably because I had so recently traversed it, and was familiar with its difficulties. I had heard and read so much concerning the desolation and elemental upheavals and violent waters of the upper valley of the Snake, that I dared not attempt to return in that

31. He had just missed Warren Gillette, and Pvts. Williamson and Moore. They arrived at the outlet of Heart Lake (Heart River), scanned the beachline for smoke, then continued down Heart River to Snake River. Had they gone up to the Rustic Group of hot springs they would have seen Everts's pitiful shelter ("a little brush shanty," according to the Helena *Daily Herald* for October 26), and had they been a few hours later they would have seen the smoke from Everts's rekindled fire. Gillette in Cockhill, p. 27.

direction. The route by the Madison Range, encumbered by the single obstruction of the mountain barrier, was much the shortest, and so, most unwisely as will hereafter appear, I adopted it.[32]

Filling my pouches with thistle-roots, I took a parting survey of the little solitude that had afforded me food and fire the preceding ten days, and with something of that melancholy feeling experienced by one who leaves his home to grapple with untried adventures, started for the nearest point on Yellowstone Lake. All that day I traveled over timber-heaps, amid tree-tops, and through thickets. At noon I took the precaution to obtain fire. With a brand which I kept alive by frequent blowing, and constant waving to and fro, at a late hour in the afternoon, faint and exhausted, I kindled a fire for the night on the only vacant spot I could find amid a dense wilderness of pines. The deep gloom of the forest, in the spectral light which revealed on all sides of me a compact and unending growth of trunks, and an impervious canopy of somber foliage; the shrieking of night-birds; the supernaturally human scream of the mountain lion;[33] the prolonged howl of the wolf, made me insensible to all other forms of suffering.

The burn on my hip was so inflamed that I could only sleep in a sitting posture. Seated with my back against a tree, the smoke from the fire almost enveloping me in its suffocating folds, I vainly tried, amid the din and uproar of this horrible serenade, to woo the drowsy god. My imagination was instinct with terror. At one moment it seemed as if, in the density of a thicket, I could see

32. Eagle Rock bridge was then at the present site of Idaho Falls, Idaho. The canyons of the Snake River that Everts refers to are south of the Jackson Hole area.

33. The cry of the mountain lion was well known to resemble that of a human. As mentioned earlier, other party members had heard its shriek "so terribly human" that for a moment they believed it to be a call from Mr. Everts. Langford's note in *Scribner's* used the old word *amiss* for lion:

> During the night we were startled by the shrill and almost human scream of an amiss or mountain lion, which sounded uncomfortably near. This terrible animal is much larger than the panther of the eastern forests, but greatly resembles it in shape, color, and ferocity. It is the terror of mountaineers, and furnishes them with the staples for many tales full of daring exploits.

Langford, "Wonders of the Yellowstone," p. 116.

A NIGHT OF TERROR

the blazing eyes of a formidable forest monster fixed upon me, preparatory to a deadly leap; at another I fancied that I heard the swift approach of a pack of yelping wolves through the distant brushwood, which in a few moments would tear me limb from limb. Whenever, by fatigue and weakness, my terrors yielded to drowsiness, the least noise roused me to a sense of the hideousness of my condition. Once, in a fitful slumber, I fell forward into the fire, and inflicted a wretched burn on my hand. Oh! with what agony I longed for day!

A bright and glorious morning succeeded the dismal night, and brought with it the conviction that I had been the victim of uncontrollable nervous excitement. I resolved henceforth to banish it altogether; and, in much better spirits than I anticipated, resumed my journey towards the lake. Another day of unceasing toil among the treetops and thickets overtook me, near sunset, standing upon a lofty headland jutting into the lake, and commanding a magnificent prospect of the mountains and valley over an immense area.[34] In front of me, at a distance of fifty miles away, in the clear blue of the horizon, rose the arrowy peaks of the three Tetons. On the right, and apparently in close proximity to the eminence I occupied, rolled the picturesque range of the Madison, scarred with clefts, ravines, gorges, and cañons, each of which glittered in the sunlight or deepened in shadow as the fitful rays of the descending luminary glanced along their varied rocky irregularities. Above where I stood were the lofty domes of Mounts Langford and Doane, marking the limits of that wonderful barrier which had so long defied human power in its efforts to subdue it.[35] Rising seemingly from the promontory which favored my vision was the familiar summit of Mount Everts [Sheridan], at the base of which I had dwelt so long, and which still seemed to hold me within its friendly shadow. All the vast country within this grand enclosure of mountains and lake, scarred and seamed with the grotesque ridges, rocky escarpments, undulating hillocks, and miniature lakes, and steaming with hot springs, produced by the volcanic forces of a former era, lay spread out before me like a vast panorama.

I doubt if distress and suffering can ever entirely obliterate all sense of natural grandeur and magnificence. Lost in the wonder and admiration

34. We can only speculate about where Everts was here. He could have been standing on the top of Flat Mountain, where his friends had watched a forest fire earlier, or on Chicken Ridge. Or he could have been on a high point somewhere along the Continental Divide south of West Thumb. His use of the word prospect here is typical for the nineteenth century, although atypical today, and that use illustrates the reason for two place names in the park: *Prospect Point* and *Prospect Peak*.

35. By "Mount Langford," Everts is probably referring to present Colter Peak. By "Mount Doane," he means an unnamed peak just north of present Colter Peak, probably the one marked "10149" on present maps. Both are in the Absaroka Range. The Washburn party had given the peaks the names used here by Everts, but the 1871 Hayden survey transferred the names *Langford* and *Doane* to their present locations farther north and left the two peaks that Everts here refers to unnamed. Arnold Hague named Colter Peak in 1885 for John Colter. Haines, *Yellowstone Story*, I, pp. 121–24.

inspired by this vast world of beauties, I nearly forgot to improve the few moments of remaining sunshine to obtain fire. With a lighted brand in my hand, I effected a most difficult and arduous descent of the abrupt and stony headland to the beach of the lake. The sand was soft and yielding. I kindled a fire, and removing the stiffened slippers from my feet, attached them to my belt, and wandered barefoot along the sandy shore to gather wood for the night. The dry, warm sand was most grateful to my lacerated and festering feet, and for a long time after my wood-pile was supplied, I sat with them uncovered. At length, conscious of the need of every possible protection from the freezing night atmosphere, I sought my belt for the slippers, and one was missing. In gathering the wood it had become detached, and was lost. Darkness was closing over the landscape, when, sorely disheartened with the thought of passing the night with one foot exposed to a freezing temperature, I commenced a search for the missing slipper. I knew I could not travel a day without it. Fearful that it had dropped into the lake, and been carried by some recurrent wave beyond recovery, my search for an hour among fallen trees and bushes, up the hill-side and along the beach, in darkness and with flaming brands, at one moment crawling on hands and feet into a brush-heap, another peering among the logs and bushes and stones, was filled with anxiety and dismay. Success at length rewarded my perseverance, and no language can describe the joy with which I drew the cause of so much distress from beneath the limb that, as I passed, had torn it from my belt. With a feeling of great relief, I now sat down in the sand, my back to a log, and listened to the dash and roar of the waves. It was a wild lullaby, but had no terrors for a worn-out man. I never passed a night of more refreshing sleep. When I awoke my fire was extinguished save a few embers, which I soon fanned into a cheerful flame. I ate breakfast with some relish, and started along the beach in pursuit of a camp, believing that if successful I should find directions what to do, and food to sustain me. The search which I was making lay in the direction of my pre-arranged route to the Madison Mountains, which I intended to approach at their lowest point of altitude.

Buoyed by the hope of finding food and counsel, and another night of undisturbed repose in the sand, I resumed my journey along the shore, and at noon found the camp last occupied by my friends on the lake.[36] I struck their trail in the sand some time before I came to it. A thorough search for food in the ground and trees revealed nothing, and no notice to apprise me of their movements could be seen.[37] A dinner-fork, which afterwards proved to be of immense service in digging roots, and a yeast-powder can, which would hold half a pint, and which I converted into a drinking-cup and dinner pot, were the only evidences that the spot had ever been visited by civilized man. "Oh!" thought I, "why did they forget to leave me food!" it never occurring to me that they might have cached it, as I have since learned they did, in several spots nearer the place of my separation from them. I left the camp in deep dejection, with the purpose of following the trail of the party

36. The camp was in the area of present West Thumb Geyser Basin, and called "Hot Spring Camp" by their party. From this point at West Thumb until Everts returns to the Yellowstone River at "the debouchure of the river," his route is unknown.

37. They had left notices and food at other places but not at this one.

THE BURNING FOREST

38. The upper part of Firehole River, in the Old Faithful area, was known in those days as "Madison River." Everts's friends had proceeded west from West Thumb toward DeLacy Creek, Kepler Cascades, and Old Faithful, which is roughly the route of the present main road.

to the Madison.[38] Carefully inspecting the faint traces left of their course of travel, I became satisfied that from some cause they had made a retrograde movement from the camp, and departed from the lake at some point farther down stream. Taking this as an indication that there were obstructions above, I commenced retracing my steps along the beach. An hour of sunshine in the afternoon enabled me to procure fire, which, in the usual manner, I carried to my camping-place. There I built a fire, and to protect myself from the wind, which was blowing violently, lashing the lake into foam, I made a bower of pine boughs, crept under it, and very soon fell asleep. How long I slept I know not, but I was aroused by the snapping and cracking of the burning foliage, to find my shelter and the adjacent forest in a broad sheet of flame. My left hand was badly burned, and my hair singed closer than a barber would have trimmed it, while making my escape from the semicircle of burning trees.[39] Among the disasters of this fire, there was none I felt more seriously than the loss of my buckle-tongue knife, my pin fish-hook, and tape fish-line.

The grandeur of the burning forest surpasses description. An immense sheet of flame, following to their tops the lofty trees of an almost impenetrable pine forest, leaping madly from top to top, and sending thousands of forked tongues a hundred feet or more athwart the midnight darkness, lighting up with lurid gloom and glare the surrounding scenery of lake and mountains, fills the beholder with mingled feelings of awe and astonishment. I never before saw anything so terribly beautiful. It was marvelous to witness the flash-like rapidity with which the flames would mount the loftiest trees. The roaring, cracking, crashing, and snapping of falling limbs and burning foliage was deafening. On, on, on traveled the destructive element, until it seemed as if the whole forest was enveloped in flame. Afar up the wood-crowned hill, the overtopping trees shot forth pinnacles and walls and streamers of arrowy fire. The entire hill-side was an ocean of glowing and surging fiery billows. Favored by the gale, the conflagration spread with lightning swiftness over an illimitable extent of country, filling the atmosphere with driving clouds of suffocating fume[s], and leaving a broad and blackened trail of spectral trunks shorn of limbs and foliage,

39. This burn was apparently severe enough to bother Everts for much of the rest of his life, as his son mentioned it to park officials in a 1961 interview. Truman Everts, Jr., stated that his father was burned "on one side" from a forest fire. Aubrey L. Haines interview with Truman Everts, Jr., August 11, 1961, audiotape number 61-3, YNP Research Library.

40. We do not know where he was nor what range he was seeing. Assuming he was remembering his trip chronology correctly, Everts must have climbed a high point near West Thumb to see this "lowest notch" in the "Madison Range." But the high points near West Thumb are largely tree-covered and do not easily allow for long distance views, so Everts might have traveled some distance before ascending his high point.

So where did he go from West Thumb? Logically, when Everts left there, he should have followed the north shore of Yellowstone Lake around to the river's outlet, but if his text is correct he did not, for surely he would have mentioned the lakeshore once or twice had he been following it. Instead he wrote of viewing unknown high peaks from unknown high ridges. In accordance with Mr. Norris's comments in note 43, this author believes that Everts struck out to the northwest from West Thumb in the direction of Mary Lake, perhaps even reaching it. From high points on this route he could have had occasional views of the southern Gallatin Range or even the Madison Range if he got high enough or far enough west, and either range would have looked light years away from him. He eventually turned back east to the Yellowstone River outlet which he calls the "debouchure [outlet] of the river."

41. Once again it is not known what hill Everts was sitting on. It could have been a high point of the Central Plateau from which he surveyed the Yellowstone River. But his chosen route was indeed the shortest way to the settlements. Had Everts been able to find the Firehole, Gibbon, or Madison rivers, he could have followed any of them down to Gilman Sawtell's ranch, established in 1868, near Henry's Lake.

smoking and burning, to mark the immense sweep of its devastation.

Resolved to search for a trail no longer, when daylight came I selected for a landmark the lowest notch in the Madison Range.[40] Carefully surveying the jagged and broken surface over which I must travel to reach it, I left the lake and pushed into the midst of its intricacies. All the day, until nearly sunset, I struggled over rugged hills, through windfalls, thickets, and matted forests, with the rock-ribbed beacon constantly in view. As I advanced it receded, as if in mockery of my toil. Night overtook me with my journey half accomplished. The precaution of obtaining fire gave me warmth and sleep, and long before daylight I was on my way. The hope of finding an easy pass into the valley of the Madison inspired me with fresh courage and determination; but long before I arrived at the base of the range, I scanned hopelessly its insurmountable difficulties. It presented to my eager vision an endless succession of inaccessible peaks and precipices, rising thousands of feet sheer and bare above the plain. No friendly gorge or gully or cañon invited such an effort as I could make to scale this rocky barrier. Oh for the faith that could remove mountains! How soon should this colossal fabric open at my approach! What a feeling of helpless despair came over me with the conviction that the journey of the last two days had been in vain! I seated myself on a rock, upon the summit of a commanding hill, and cast my eyes along the only route which now seemed tenable—down the Yellowstone [River].[41] How many dreary miles of forest and mountain

THE GHOSTLY COUNSELLOR

filled the terrible panorama! I thought that before accepting this discouraging alternative I would spend a day in search for a pass. Twenty miles at most would take me into the Madison Valley, and thirty more restore me to friends who had abundance. Supposing that I should find plenty of thistles, I had left the lake with [but] a small supply, and that was entirely spent. I looked in vain for them where I then was.

While I was thus considering whether to remain and search for a passage or return to the Yellowstone, I experienced one of those strange hallucinations which many of my friends have misnamed insanity, but which to me was Providence. An old clerical friend, for whose character and counsel I had always cherished peculiar regard, in some unaccountable manner seemed to be standing before me, charged with advice which would relieve my perplexity. I seemed to hear him say, as if in a voice and with the manner of authority:—

"Go back immediately, as rapidly as your strength will permit. There is no food here, and the idea of scaling these rocks is madness."

"Doctor," I rejoined, "the distance is too great. I cannot live to travel it."

"Say not so. Your life depends upon the effort. Return at once. Start now, lest your resolution falter. Travel as fast and as far as possible—it is your only chance."

"Doctor, I am rejoiced to meet you in this hour of distress, but doubt the wisdom of your counsel. I am within seventy miles of Virginia [City]. Just over these rocks, a few miles away, I shall find friends. My shoes are nearly worn out, my clothes are in tatters, and my strength is almost overcome. As a last trial, it seems to me I can but attempt to scale this mountain or perish in the effort, if God so wills."

"Don't think of it. Your power of endurance will carry you through. I will accompany you. Put your trust in heaven. Help yourself and God will help you."

Overcome by these and other persuasions, and delighted with the idea of having a traveling companion,[42] I plodded my way over the route I had come, intending at a certain point to change it so as to strike the river at the foot of the lake.[43] Stopping after a few miles of travel, I had no difficulty in procuring fire, and passed a comfortable night. When I resumed my journey the next day the sun was just rising. Whenever I was disposed, as was often the case, to question the wisdom of the change of routes, my old friend appeared to be near with words of encouragement, but his reticence on other subjects both surprised and annoyed me. I was impressed at times, during the entire journey, with the belief that my return was a fatal error, and [that] if my deliverance had failed [I] should have perished with that conviction. Early this day I deflected from my old route and took my course for the foot of the lake, with the hope, by constant travel, to reach it the next day. The distance was greater than I anticipated. Nothing is more deceptive than distance in these high latitudes. At the close of each of the two succeeding days, my point of destination was seemingly as far from me as at the moment I took leave of the Madison Range,[44] and when, cold and hungry, on the afternoon of the fourth day, I gathered the first food I had eaten in nearly five days, and lay down by my fire near the debouchure of the river, I had nearly abandoned all hope of escape.[45]

At day-break I was on the trail down the river.[46] The thought I had adopted from the first, "I will not perish in this wilderness," often revived my sinking spirits, when, from faintness and exhaustion, I felt but little desire for life. Once, while struggling through a field of tangled

42. It is apparent that at this point Everts was no longer operating "with a full deck." Lack of food, cold weather, and general hardship had combined to cause hallucinations.

43. Everts knew that Yellowstone River ran out of Yellowstone Lake because his party had crossed the river earlier, at Nez Perce Ford six miles below the lake.

In the following little-known lines, Park superintendent P.W. Norris noted that Everts's decision to retrace his steps, advice given by Everts's ghostly counselor, was a wise and correct one. But just as interesting here is Norris's assertion that Everts first tried to proceed west to Mary Lake (discovering it in the process) before he turned north to retrace his original route. Because Norris was a close personal friend of Everts, we must view these comments as more credible than most secondhand versions of Everts's story. Indeed Everts himself has here stated that he first tried to go west before receiving the "advice" to turn north. Did Norris and Everts discuss Everts's route later, as seems possible, or did Norris merely presume the Mary's Lake material from Everts's written account? We do not know, but here are Norris's comments:

> The route by which Evarts [sic] attempted to leave the park was via Morey's [sic— Mary's] Lake (which he discovered), Forks of the Fire hole rivers and Gibbon's pass of the Madison range, which, as usual with mountain passes is less visible as you approach it. As this is the route by which [Julius] Beltizer and myself returned through snow [which reached] to our saddle girths, Sept 2, 1875, as noted in No. 25 of the Suburban, I unhesitatingly declare the above advice [from Everts' ghostly counselor] . . . to descend the Yellowstone was wise, and in his weak and destitute condition all that saved him.

Norris in "Meanderings of a Mountaineer . . . ," following the poem, "Keep Your Family My Rural Neighbor."

44. Probably rolling ridges on the Central Plateau or the Madison Plateau. It is doubt-

trunks which seemed interminable, at one of the pauses I found myself seriously considering whether it was not preferable to die there than renew the effort to proceed. I felt that all attempt to escape was but a bitter prolongation of the agony of dissolution. A seeming whisper in the air, "While there is life there is hope; take courage," broke the delusion, and I clambered on. I did not forget to improve [use] the mid-day sun to procure fire. Sparks from the lighted brands had burned my hands and crisped the nails of my fingers, and the smoke from them [and the sun itself] had tanned my face to the complexion of an Indian. While passing through an opening in the forest I found the tip of a gull's wing; it was fresh. I made a fire upon the spot, mashed the bones with a stone, and consigning them to my camp kettle, the yeast-powder box, made half a pint of delicious broth. The remainder of that day and the night ensuing were given to sleep.

I lost all sense of time. Days and nights came and went, and were numbered only by the growing consciousness that I was gradually starving. I felt no hunger, did not eat to appease appetite, but to renew strength. I experienced but little pain. The gaping sores on my feet, the severe burn on my hip, the festering crevices at the joints of my fingers, all terrible in appearance, had ceased to give me the least concern. The roots which supplied my food had suspended the digestive power of the stomach, and their fibres were packed in it in a matted, compact mass.

Not so with my hours of slumber. They were visited by the most luxurious dreams. I would ap-

ful Everts got as far west as the Madison Range, which is west of present West Yellowstone, Montana, but he might have seen that range from high ridges if he took the Mary's Lake route.

45. Everts was apparently near present Fishing Bridge on the west side of Yellowstone River.

46. Except for the fact that he was on the west side of the river, Everts was now following the old route of the Washburn party, along which he himself had traveled earlier. The party had forded to the east side .8 mile above Mud Volcano at Nez Perce Ford.

parently visit the most gorgeously decorated restaurants of New York and Washington; sit down
to immense tables spread with the most appetiz-
ing viands; partake of the richest oyster stews and
plumpest pies; engage myself in the labor and
preparation of curious dishes, and with them fill
range upon range of elegantly furnished tables
until they fairly groaned beneath the accumulated
dainties prepared by my own hands. Frequently
the entire night would seem to have been spent in
getting up a sumptuous dinner. I would realize
the fatigue of roasting, boiling, baking, and fabri-
cating the choicest dishes known to the modern
cuisine, and in my disturbed slumbers would enjoy with epicurean relish the food thus furnished
even to repletion. Alas! there was more luxury
than life in these somnolent vagaries.

It was a cold, gloomy day when I arrived in the
vicinity of the falls.[47] The sky was overcast and
the snow-capped peaks rose chilly and bleak
through the biting atmosphere. The moaning of
the wind through the pines, mingling with the
sullen roar of the falls, was strangely in unison
with my own saddened feelings. I had no heart to
gaze upon a scene which a few weeks before had
inspired me with rapture and awe. One moment
of sunshine was of more value to me than all the
marvels amid which I was famishing. But the sun
had hid[den] his face and denied me all hope of
obtaining fire. The only alternative was to seek
shelter in a thicket. I penetrated the forest a long
distance before finding one that suited me. Breaking and crowding my way into its very midst,
I cleared a spot large enough to recline upon,

47. Lower Falls of the Yellowstone River,
308 feet high, and Upper Falls, 109 feet high.
His party had passed them earlier.

interlaced the surrounding brushwood, gathered the fallen foliage into a bed, and lay down with a prayer for sleep and forgetfulness. Alas! neither came. The coldness increased through the night. Constant friction with my hands and unceasing beating with my legs and feet saved me from freezing. It was the most terrible night of my journey, and when, with the early dawn, I pulled myself into a standing posture, it was to realize that my right arm was partially paralyzed, and my limbs so stiffened with cold as to be almost immovable. Fearing lest paralysis should suddenly seize upon the entire system, I literally dragged myself through the forest to the river.[48] Seated near the verge of the great cañon below the falls, I anxiously awaited the appearance of the sun. That great luminary never looked so beautiful as when, a few moments afterwards, he emerged from the clouds and exposed his glowing beams to the concentrated powers of my lens. I kindled a mighty flame, fed it with every dry stick and broken tree-top I could find, and without motion, and almost without sense, remained beside it several hours. The great falls of the Yellowstone were roaring within three hundred yards, and the awful cañon yawned almost at my feet; but they had lost all charm for me. In fact, I regarded them as enemies which had lured me to destruction, and felt a sullen satisfaction in morbid indifference.

My old friend and advisor, whose presence I had felt more than seen the last few days, now forsook me altogether. But I was not alone. By some process which I was too weak to solve, my arms, legs, and stomach were transformed into so many

48. Everts must mean to the brink of the canyon here, for a little later he says the "great falls" (Lower Falls) is roaring within three hundred yards of him, and in his fatigued state he would not have gone down to the brink of the river. Probably he was somewhere near present Lookout Point.

The term "great falls" was used in accounts of that era in contradistinction to "little falls," a prospectors' term which referred to Tower Fall farther downstream. Aubrey L. Haines to Tom Tankersley, October 17, 1994.

IMAGINARY COMPANIONS

traveling companions. Often for hours I would plod along conversing with these imaginary friends. Each had his peculiar wants which he expected me to supply. The stomach was importunate in his demand for a change of diet—complained incessantly of the roots I fed him, their present effect and more remote consequences. I would try to silence him with promises, beg him to wait a few days, and when this failed of the quiet I desired, I would seek to intimidate him by declaring, as a sure result of negligence, our inability to reach home alive. All to no purpose—he tormented me with his fretful humors through the entire journey. The others would generally concur with him in these fancied altercations. The legs implored me for rest, and the arms complained that I gave them too much to do. Troublesome as they were, it was a pleasure to realize their presence. I worked for them, too, with right good will, doing many things for their seeming comfort which, had I felt myself alone, would have remained undone. They appeared to be perfectly helpless of themselves; would do nothing for me or for each other. I often wondered, while they ate and slept so much, that they did not aid in gathering wood and kindling fires. As a counterpoise to their own inertia, whenever they discovered languor in me on necessary occasions, they were not wanting in words of encouragement and cheer. I recall as I write an instance where, by prompt and timely interposition, the representative of the stomach saved me from a death of dreadful agony. One day I came to a small stream issuing from a spring of mild temperature on the hillside, swarming with minnows. I caught some with my hands and ate them raw. To my taste they were delicious. But the stomach refused them, accused me of attempting to poison him, and would not be reconciled until I had emptied my pouch of the few fish I had put there for future use. Those fish that I ate made me very sick. Poisoned by the mineral in the water, had I glutted my appetite with them as I intended, I should doubtless have died in the wilderness, in excruciating torment.[49]

A gradual mental introversion grew upon me as physical weakness increased. The grand and

49. It is doubtful that the water was poisoned, or else fish probably could not have lived. It is more likely that Everts's stomach simply could not take the fish after a forced diet of thistles. It is not known what stream and spring he had happened upon, but it runs into the Yellowstone River from the west side.

massive scenery which, on the upward journey, had aroused every enthusiastic impulse of my nature, was now tame and spiritless. My thoughts were turned in upon myself—upon the dreadful fate which apparently lay just before me—and the possible happiness of the existence beyond. All doubt of immortality fled in the light of present realities. So vivid were my conceptions of the future that at times I longed for death, not less as the beginning of happiness than as a release from misery. Led on by these reflections, I would recall the varied incidents of my journey—my escape from the lion, from fire, my return from the Madison Range—and in all of them I saw how much I had been indebted to that mysterious protection which comes only from the throne of the Eternal. And yet, starving, foot-sore, half blind, worn to a skeleton, was it surprising that I lacked the faith needful to buoy me above the dark waters of despair, which I now felt were closing around me?

In less serious moods, as I struggled along, my thoughts would revert to the single being on whom my holiest affections centred—my daughter. What a tie was that to bind me to life! Oh! could I be restored to her for a single hour, long enough for parting counsel and blessing, it would be joy unspeakable! Long hours of painful travel were relieved of physical suffering by this absorbing agony of the mind, which, when from my present stand-point I contrast it with the personal calamities of my exile, swells into mountains.

To return from this digression. At many of the streams on my route I spent hours in endeavoring to catch trout, with a hook fashioned from the rim of my broken spectacles, but in no instance with success. The tackle was defective. The country was full of game in great variety. I saw large herds of deer, elk, antelope, occasionally a bear, and many smaller animals. Numerous flocks of ducks, geese, swans, and pelicans inhabited the lakes and rivers. But with no means of killing them, their presence was a perpetual aggravation. At all the [previous] camps of our company I stopped and recalled many pleasant incidents associated with them.

One afternoon, when approaching "Tower Falls," I came upon a large hollow tree, which, from the numerous tracks surrounding it, and the matted foliage in the cavity, I recognized as the den of a bear. It was a most inviting couch. Gathering a needful supply of wood and brush, I lighted a circle of piles around the tree, crawled into the nest, and passed a night of unbroken slumber. I rose the next morning to find that during the night the fires had communicated with the adjacent forest, and burned a large space in all directions, doubtless intimidating the rightful proprietor of the nest, and saving me from another midnight adventure.

At "Tower Falls" I spent the first half of a day in capturing a grasshopper, and the remainder in a fruitless effort to catch a mess of trout. In the agony of disappointment, I resolved to fish no more.[50] A spirit of rebellion seized me. I determined that thistles should thenceforth be my only sustenance. "Why is it," I asked of myself, "that in the midst of abundance, every hour meeting with objects which would restore strength and vigor and energy, every moment contriving some device

50. In a subsequent interview, Everts told Samuel Langhorne that he had caught "two large fish" at some point on his adventure, but, if it happened, Everts's own narrative does not mention it except in this indirect way. Likewise there are inconsistencies in the accounts of whether or not Everts ate grasshoppers, one stating that they would not stay on his stomach. There are also two mentions of him unsuccessfully chasing a toad for two days. Helena *Daily Herald*, October 26, 28, 1870. See also the G.L. Henderson quote at note 11 in the Afterword.

to procure the nourishment my wasting frame required, I should meet with these repeated and discouraging failures?["] Thoughts of the early teaching of a pious mother suppressed these feelings. Oh! how often have the recollections of a loved New England home, and the memories of a happy childhood, cheered my sinking spirits, and dissipated the gathering gloom of despair! There were thoughts and feelings and mental anguishes without number, that visited me during my period of trial, that never can be known to any but my God and myself. Bitter as was my experience, it was not unrelieved by some of the most precious moments I have ever known.

Soon after leaving "Tower Falls," I entered the open country. Pine forests and windfalls were changed for sage brush and desolation, with occasional tracts of stinted verdure, barren hillsides, exhibiting here and there an isolated clump of dwarf trees, and ravines filled with the rocky *debris* of adjacent mountains. My first camp on this part of the route, for the convenience of getting wood, was made near the summit of a range of towering foot-hills. Towards morning a storm of wind and snow nearly extinguished my fire. I became very cold; the storm was still raging when I arose, and the ground white with snow. I was perfectly bewildered, and had lost my course of travel. No visible object, seen through the almost blinding storm, reassured me, and there was no alternative but to find the river[51] and take my direction from its current. Fortunately, after a few hours of stumbling and scrambling among rocks and over crests, I came to the precipitous side of

51. He was heading back to the Yellowstone River which is still in its canyon in and below the Tower Fall area.

DESCENDING THE PRECIPICE

the cañon through which it ran, and with much labor, both of hands and feet, descended it to the margin. I drank copiously of its pure waters, and sat beside it for a long time, waiting for the storm to abate, so that I could procure fire. The day wore on without any prospect of a termination of the storm. Chilled through, my tattered clothing saturated, I saw before me a night of horrors unless I returned to my fire. The scramble up the side of the rocky cañon, in many places nearly perpendicular, was the hardest work of my journey. Often while clinging to the jutting rocks with hands and feet, to reach a shelving projection, my grasp would unclose and I would slide many feet down the sharp declivity. It was night when, sore from the bruises I had received, I reached my fire; the storm, still raging, had nearly extinguished it. I found a few embers in the ashes, and with much difficulty kindled a flame. Here, on this bleak mountain side, as well as I now remember, I must have passed two nights beside the fire, in the storm. Many times during each night I crawled to the little clump of trees to gather wood, and brush, and the broken limbs of fallen tree-tops. All the sleep I obtained was snatched from the intervals which divided these labors. It was so harassed with frightful dreams as to afford little rest. I remember, before I left this camp, stripping up my sleeves to look at my shrunken arms. Flesh and blood had apparently left them. The skin clung to the bones like wet parchment. A child's hand could have clasped them from wrist to shoulder. "Yet," thought I, "it is death to remain; I cannot perish in this wilderness."

Taking counsel of this early formed resolution, I hobbled on my course through the snow, which was rapidly disappearing before the rays of the warm sun. Well knowing that I should find no thistles in the open country, I had filled my pouches with them before leaving the forest.[52] My supply was running low, and there were yet

52. Today Everts Thistle grows abundantly in the open meadows of northern Yellowstone. Park plant specialist Don Despain says he thinks Everts was simply mistaken.

several days of heavy mountain travel between me and Boteler's ranch.[53] With the most careful economy, it could last but two or three days longer. I saw the necessity of placing myself and imaginary companions upon allowance. The conflict which ensued with the stomach, when I announced this resolution, required great firmness to carry through. I tried wheedling and coaxing and promising; failing in these, I threatened to part company with a comrade so unreasonable, and he made no further complaint.

Two or three days before I was found, while ascending a steep hill, I fell from exhaustion into the sage brush, without the power to rise. Unbuckling my belt, as was my custom, I soon fell asleep. I have no idea of the time I slept, but upon awakening I fastened my belt, scrambled to my feet, and pursued my journey. As night drew on I selected a camping-place, gathered wood into a heap, and felt for my lens to procure fire. It was gone. If the earth had yawned to swallow me I would not have been more terrified. The only chance for life was lost. The last hope had fled. I seemed to feel the grim messenger who had been so long pursuing me knocking at the portals of my heart as I lay down by the side of the wood-pile, and covered myself with limbs and sage-brush, with the dreadful conviction that my struggle for life was over, and that I should rise no more. The floodgates of misery seemed now to be opened, and it rushed in living tide upon my soul. With the rapidity of lightning, I ran over every event of my life. Thoughts doubled and trebled upon me, until I saw, as if in vision, the entire past

53. Bottler's ranch, owned by three Bottler brothers and their mother, had been settled by 1868 in present Paradise Valley, Montana. Everts's party had stayed there on their way into the park area.

of my existence. It was all before me, as if painted with a sunbeam, and all seemingly faded like the phantoms of a vivid dream.

As calmness returned, reason resumed her empire. Fortunately, the weather was comfortable. I summoned all the powers of my memory, thought over every foot of the day's travel, and concluded that the glass must have become detached from my belt while sleeping. Five long miles over the hills must be retraced to regain it. There was no alternative, and before daylight I had staggered over half the distance. I found the lens on the spot where I had slept. No incident of my journey brought with it more of joy and relief.

Returning to the camp of the previous night, I lighted the pile I had prepared, and lay down for a night of rest. It was very cold, and towards morning commenced snowing. With difficulty I kept the fire alive. Sleep was impossible. When daylight came, I was impressed with the idea that I must go on despite the storm. A flash—momentary but vivid—came over me, that I should be saved. Snatching a lighted brand, I started through the storm. In the afternoon the storm abated and the sun shone at intervals. Coming to a small clump of trees, I set to work to prepare camp. I laid the brand down which I preserved with so much care, to pick up a few dry sticks with which to feed it, until I could collect wood for a camp-fire, and in the few minutes thus employed it expired. I sought to revive it, but every spark was gone. Clouds obscured the sun, now near the horizon, and the prospect of another night of exposure without fire became fearfully imminent.

I sat down with my lens and the last remaining piece of touchwood I possessed to catch a gleam of sunshine, feeling that my life depended on it. In a few moments the cloud passed, and with trembling hands I presented the little disk to the face of the glowing luminary. Quivering with excitement lest a sudden cloud should interpose, a moment passed before I could hold the lens steadily enough to concentrate a burning focus. At length it came. The little thread of smoke curled gracefully upwards from the Heaven-lighted spark, which, a few moments afterwards, diffused with warmth and comfort my desolate lodgings.

I resumed my journey the next morning, with the belief that I should make no more fires with my lens. I must save a brand, or perish. The day was raw and gusty; an east wind, charged with storm, penetrated my nerves with irritating keenness. After walking a few miles the storm came on, and a coldness unlike any other I had ever felt seized me. It entered all my bones. I attempted to build a fire, but could not make it burn. Seizing a brand, I stumbled blindly on, stopping within the shadow of every rock and clump to renew energy for a final conflict for life. A solemn conviction that death was near, that at each pause I made my limbs would refuse further service, and that I should sink helpless and dying in my path, overwhelmed me with terror. Amid all this tumult of the mind, I felt that I had done all that man could do. I knew that in two or three days more I could effect my deliverance, and I derived no little satisfaction from the thought that, as I was now in the broad trail,[54] my remains

54. Decades of travel by Indians on the Great Bannock Trail, likely coupled with the passing of Everts's party earlier and a few prospectors trekking towards what would become Cooke City, had resulted in a wide and visible trail through the area of the present Cut.

THE RESCUE

would be found, and my friends relieved of doubts as to my fate. Once only the thought flashed across my mind that I should be saved, and I seemed to hear a whispered command to "Struggle on." Groping along the side of a hill, I became suddenly sensible of a sharp reflection, as of burnished steel. Looking up, through half-closed eyes, two rough but kindly faces met my gaze.

"Are you Mr. Everts?"

"Yes. All that is left of him."

"We have come for you."

"Who sent you?"

"Judge Lawrence[55] and other friends."

55. The Helena law partner of another member of the Washburn party, Cornelius Hedges.

56. Samuel Langhorne, who talked directly to Jack Baronett about the rescue, wrote an account of it for Helena newspapers. Langhorne's account, like Baronett's reproduced at the end of this book, does not give Everts credit for quite as much conversation at the time of his deliverance as Everts would have us believe. Langhorne had this from Baronett:

Barnett [sic] . . . says he was traveling on the side of a tall mountain, and described an object on the opposite side of another mountain, walking along and occasionally stooping down behind rocks, evidently seeking shelter from the wind, as it had been snowing and was bitterly cold. The mountain was rough and covered with large boulders, and the object would dodge about from one to the other to gain protection from the chilling wind. He (Barnett) [sic] immediately started across the intervening space, and when he got within ten or fifteen feet, Mr. Everts (for it was him) threw up his hands, but could not articulate anything distinctly. Barnett [sic] then took him on his shoulders and bore him down in the valley to camp, and made him some tea; then for the first time he ejaculated "Thank God, I am safe."

"The Finding of Hon. T.C. Everts," Helena *Daily Herald*, October 26, 1870.

A third source agrees. Leander Frary's letter to the newspaper states that at the time of the rescue "the vital spark [in Mr. Everts] was just alive, and that is all—[he] being unconscious, and speechless." "More About Mr. Everts," Helena *Daily Herald*, October 22, 1870.

57. Jack Baronett, a soldier of fortune, and George A. Pritchett, a prospector. See the Afterword for their individual accounts of the rescue.

58. The "Turkey Pen" cabin, then located 1.8 miles east of the present Roosevelt Arch at Gardiner, Montana. It had been built there on the Yellowstone River by prospectors, probably in 1867.

It is not known who all the men were who ministered to Everts, but one of them

"God bless him, and them, and you! I am saved!" and with these words, powerless of further effort, I fell forward into the arms of my preservers, in a state of unconsciousness. I was saved.[56] On the very brink of the river which divides the known from the unknown, strong arms snatched me from the final plunge, and kind ministrations wooed me back to life.

Baronet and Prichette,[57] my two preservers, by the usual appliances, soon restored me to consciousness, made a camp upon the spot, and while one went to Fort Ellis, a distance of seventy miles, to return with remedies to restore digestion and an ambulance to convey me to that post, the other sat by my side, and with all the care, sympathy, and solicitude of a brother, ministered to my frequent necessities. In two days I was sufficiently recovered in strength to be moved twenty miles down the trail to the cabin of some miners who were prospecting in that vicinity.[58] From these men I received every possible attention which their humane and generous natures could devise. A good bed was provided, game was killed to make broth, and the best stores of their larder placed at my command. For four days, at a time when every day's labor was invaluable in their pursuit, they abandoned their work to aid in my restoration. Owing to the protracted inaction of the [my] system, and the long period which must transpire before Prichette's return with remedies, my friends had serious doubts of my recovery.

The night after my arrival at the cabin, while suffering the most excruciating agony, and thinking that I had only been saved to die among friends, a loud knock was heard at the cabin door. An old man in mountain costume entered—a hunter, whose life was spent among the mountains. He was on his way to find a brother. He listened to the story of my sufferings, and tears rapidly coursed each other down his rough, weather-beaten face. But when he was told of my present necessity, brightening in a moment, he exclaimed:

"Why, Lord bless you, if that is all, I have the very remedy you need. In two hours' time all shall be well with you."

He left the cabin, returning in a moment with a sack filled with the fat of a bear which he had killed a few hours before. From this he rendered out a pint measure of oil. I drank the whole of it. It proved to be the needed remedy, and the next day, freed from pain, with appetite and digestion re-established, I felt that good food and plenty of it were only necessary for an early recovery.

In a day or two I took leave of my kind friends, with a feeling of regret at parting, and of gratitude for their kindness as enduring as life. Meeting the carriage on my way, I proceeded to Boseman [sic], where I remained among old friends, who gave me every attention until my health was sufficiently restored to allow me to return to my home at Helena.

My heartfelt thanks are due to the members of the Expedition, all of whom devoted seven, and some of them twelve days to the search for me before they left Yellowstone Lake; and to Judge Lawrence, of Helena, and the friends who

was George Huston, as G.L. Henderson has stated. And we also have P.W. Norris's account (below) of his conversations with Jack Baronett for clues as to who these men were.

Moreover, Norris fleshes out what Everts looked like when found and underscores Baronett's opinion that Everts would not have made it without the rescue: Attended by Barronette [sic], I, in 1875, visited the place where Everts was found. It is beside the now abandoned Sheep Eater Shoshone trail from the mouth of Gardiner [sic] River to the Forks of the Yellowstone, and some three miles [from] where Barronette [sic] afterwards built his cabin in the latter place. He has no doubt of the entire truth of Everts' narrative, and says that in all his wanderings . . . he never saw so forlorn a looking human being as was Evarts [sic] when found. A few tattered rags upon an emaciated skeleton, frozen, scalded, singed and festered into the semblance of a two-legged animal, hideous beyond description, who could not by any possibility have crossed Gardiner's River, the mountain spurs and cañons in the 50 long mountain miles to Bottler's, and only a miracle saved him. . . . Of those active in saving him, Judge Lawrence, once of Jackson, Michigan, died at Helena soon after my return from the region in 1875. The old mountaineer who furnished the oil was killed in the Stillwater valley by the Sioux during the past summer, and the sergeant of the escort who conveyed him to Fort Ellis fell under Gibbon in the Judith Badlands. [George] Huston is still on the East fork of the Yellowstone. All known of Prichette I have from Barronette [sic] who says that he was an old mountaineer who soon after getting the $600 reward wandered via the Kootenay and Saskatchwan [sic] in British America to Peace river branch of the McKensey where he is supposed to have been killed, as a large reward offered by Barronette [sic] for some trace of him failed to find it.

cooperated with him in the offer of reward which sent Baronet and Prichette [sic] to my rescue.

My narrative is finished. In the course of events the time is not far distant when the wonders of the Yellowstone will be made accessible to all lovers of sublimity, grandeur, and novelty in natural scenery, and its majestic waters become the abode of civilization and refinement; and when that arrives, I hope, in happier mood and under more auspicious circumstances, to revisit scenes fraught for me with such thrilling interest; to ramble along the glowing beach of Bessie Lake; to sit down amid the hot springs under the shadow of Mount Everts; to thread unscared the mazy forests, retrace the dreary journey to the Madison Range, and with enraptured fancy gaze upon the mingled glories and terrors of the great falls and marvelous cañon, and to enjoy, in happy contrast with the trials they recall, their power to delight, elevate, and overwhelm the mind with wondrous and majestic beauty.

Norris, "Meanderings . . . ," "Note" to letter 46.

This fascinating piece of text also claims that George Pritchett collected a $600 reward for finding Everts that Baronett never got. Although historian Aubrey Haines believes that this was nothing more than frontier gossip, we have no proof either way. Haines to Tom Tankersley, October 17, 1994.

AFTERWORD

Truman Everts was eventually rescued
some fifty miles north of the point from which he
became lost. Realizing that his party had probably
gone on without him, he stumbled those many
miles northward to a hillside west of present Crescent Hill, where two mountaineers found him after fifteen days' search. The two mountaineers,
Jack Baronett and George Pritchett,[1] had been
sent into the country expressly for that purpose.

Everts's primary rescuer, Collins John H.
"Jack" Baronett (1829–1901), was a fabulous character. Born in Scotland, he traveled with his seafaring father to exotic places all over the world before locating in the upper Yellowstone country in
1864 to prospect for gold. In 1871, he built the
first bridge across the Yellowstone River in the
present park and operated it as a toll bridge. That
bridge plus his long presence in the area resulted
in the naming of Baronette Peak for him in 1878,
misspelled though it was. He was to help P.W.
Norris recover the bones of Custer's scout Lonesome Charley Reynolds in 1877, to guide General
Philip Sheridan and many other VIPs through
Yellowstone in the early 1880s, to become a park

1. Accompanied, at least initially, by two
Crow Indians, according to Helena *Daily
Herald* for October 21, 1870.

51

scout in 1885, and even once to be considered for the park superintendency. In later life he lived in Livingston, Montana, but always continued searching for gold. A traveler Baronett guided described him as being

> of medium stature, broad-shouldered, very straight and built like Longfellow's ship, for "strength and speed." Eyes black as a panther's and as keen and sharp. He speaks well, using good English, and his manner is mild, gentle and honest; is proud of his knowledge of the mountains and his skill with the rifle.

Superintendent Norris stated that Baronett "reached Helena the day the reward was offered for Everts," and from there Baronett and Pritchett set out to find the unfortunate lost man.[2]

Baronett's own story of the rescue of Everts, which occurred on October 16, 1870, is fascinating:

> On the thirty-eighth day that he was lost there was icy sleet falling ... barely making the ground white; but I noticed that my dog had found some kind of trail. By looking closely, I saw that something had dragged itself ... upon the ground. I decided that some hunter had wounded a bear and that it was trying to make its way up the mountains, and out of curiosity I followed on. When I had trailed the wounded bear for a mile or more, my dog began to growl, and looking across a small cañon [the Cut of present maps] to the mountain side beyond, I saw a black object upon the ground.

2. Biographical information on Baronett is from Lee H. Whittlesey, *Wonderland Nomenclature: A History of the Place Names of Yellowstone National Park* (Helena: Montana Historical Society microfiche), 1988, pp. 57–61.

Yes, sure enough, there was Bruin. My first impulse was to shoot him from where I stood, but as he was going so slowly I saw I should have no difficulty in overtaking him, and crossed over to where he was. When I got near it, I found it was not a bear, and for my life could not tell what it was. It did not look like an animal that I had seen, and it was certainly not a human being. It never occurred to me that it was Everts. I went up close to the object; it was making a low groaning noise, crawling along upon its knees and elbows, and trying to drag itself up the mountain. Then it suddenly occurred to me that it was the object of my search. I spoke his name, but he paid no attention to the sound of my voice. I stooped down and easily lifted him with one hand. Poor fellow, he was nothing but a shadow! His flesh was all gone; the bones protruded through the skin on the balls of his feet and thighs. His fingers looked like bird's claws. I carried him down to the Gardiner [sic] River, built a fire, made some tea, and gave him a spoonful. For many days and nights I watched over him, giving him a spoonful of nourishment at a time. He was constantly delirious.[3]

Baronett later pointed out the rescue spot to General W.E. Strong and told Strong the story. He had found Everts with the "clothing nearly stripped and worn from his person, which was reduced to skin and bones; hair long, and matted with dirt; eyesight nearly gone; unable to speak; and crawling on hands and feet among

3. Jack Baronett, as told to Theodore Gerrish, *Life in the World's Wonderland* (no place, no publisher, 1887), pp. 237–39.

the rocks, looking for grasshoppers and bugs for food."[4] Baronett stated that he killed a mountain lion where he found Mr. Everts and thought that the lion was tracking the unfortunate man.[5]

"Yellowstone Jack" Baronett carried Everts, who may have weighed no more than fifty pounds, to a place where a fire could be kindled, and there warmed him with some tea. The two mountaineers then took the emaciated man to a cabin near present Turkey Pen Peak, and Baronett ministered to him while Pritchett rode to Fort Ellis (present Bozeman, Montana) to get an ambulance and a doctor.

We know less about Pritchett than about Baronett, but we know he affirmed the story of the rescue more than once. In 1883, as she was leaving the park, traveler Margaret Andrews Cruikshank met Pritchett on the train between Cinnabar and Livingston, Montana. Overhearing Cruikshank's story of how Truman Everts had been rescued by Baronett and Pritchett, Pritchett exclaimed, "That's so, every word of it, for I was one of the men that found him!"[6]

Pritchett's account of the rescue also affirmed the story. It appeared in a Helena newspaper less than a week later.

We have found Mr. Everts. He is alive and safe, but very low in flesh. It seems difficult to realize the fact that he lived, but nevertheless it is so. We sent a messenger to this post for a surgeon, and afterwards I started with a fresh horse to meet him, but did not do so, and came on here: the messenger had left about an hour before I arrived

4. General W.E. Strong, in Richard A. Bartlett, ed., *A Trip to the Yellowstone National Park in July, August, and September, 1875* (Norman: University of Oklahoma Press, 1968), pp. 100–101.

5. "The Lost and Found," Helena *Daily Herald*, October 28, 1870.

6. Margaret Andrews Cruikshank, "Notes on the Yellowstone Park by M.A.C.," unpublished ms., August, 1883, p. 56, YNP Library.

with an ambulance by the wagon road,[7] and I missed him. I return tomorrow.

I understand that the messenger who came here in advance of me, sent [someone] or went to Helena to apprise the friends of Mr. Everts of his safety, and may exaggerate his condition, but I think you need not give yourselves the least uneasiness, as he has all the attention possible under the circumstances, and when the surgeon gets there he will be all right.

We found him on the 16 inst., on the summit of the first big mountain beyond Warm Spring Creek [Tower Creek], about seventy-five miles from this fort. He says he subsisted all this time on one snow bird, two small minnows, and the wing of a bird which he found and mashed between two stones, and made some broth in a yeast powder can. This was all, with the exception of thistle roots (of which he had a fair supply) he has subsisted on.

He lost his mare, saddle, gun and cantenas the first day out, and was left without fishing tackle or matches; but after making his bed over warm holes for several nights he thought he might produce fire from his opera glass, and did so. He lost both his knives. During his wanderings he saw no human beings, neither whites nor Indians, until we found him.[8]

At the time of his rescue, in addition to his loss of weight, Everts had lost his shoes plus a pair of makeshift sandals, and the balls of his frostbitten feet were thus worn to the bone. His thigh, having been earlier scalded by steam from hot springs,

7. For the story of this rescue mission, see Harry Horr, "Harry Horr's Hot Spring Claim," Bozeman *Avant Courier* (Montana), January 11, 1883.

8. "The Long-Lost Found," Helena *Daily Herald*, October 21, 1870.

9. G.L. Henderson, "Park Notes," *Livingston Enterprise*, February 5, 1887; Henderson, "Haynes' Winter Expedition," Helena *Independent*, February 6, 1887. Henderson stated here that Everts was rescued by four men: George Huston, John Evans, W. Ward, and Jack Baronett. Huston was certainly involved (see note 57 above), as was George Pritchett, but nothing more is known of Evans and Ward.

Everts's denial of insanity was published in "Letter from Mr. Everts," Helena *Daily Herald*, October 22, 1870. But Henderson, Baronett, Samuel Langhorne, Olin Wheeler, and Henry Gannett all said otherwise. Langhorne, who interviewed both Everts and Baronett after the rescue, stated that initially "his mind wandered most of the time for some days, but a limited diet of antelope tea and warm drinks gradually restored him, until he was able to give, in a disjointed manner, the way he became lost and his subsequent trials." Wheeler noted later that "he became partially deranged, but was eventually nursed back to mind and health." Olin D. Wheeler, *The Yellowstone National Park* (St. Paul: Northern Pacific Railroad, 1901), p. 16. Baronett, as noted earlier, stated that Everts was "constantly delirious." And Henry Gannett of the Hayden surveys was also a believer in Everts's short-term lunacy, writing in 1878 that Everts's hardships rendered him "temporarily insane." Gannett in F.V. Hayden, *12th Annual Report . . .* , pt. II (Washington: GPO, 1883), p. 466.

Langhorne stated that when found, Everts "did not remember how long he had been without a fire." "The Finding of Hon. T.C. Everts," Helena *Daily Herald*, October 26, 1870.

10. Just as W.E. Strong, P.W. Norris, S. Langhorne, and probably others had been.

was similarly exposed, and other areas of his body were seared and blackened. All in all he was a throughly wasted and irrational being. Chronicler G.L. Henderson, Jack Baronett, and others all stated later that Everts was "insane" when found, but Everts himself denied that.[9]

Most serious of all was a total upsetting of Everts's digestive processes caused by his forced diet of the fibrous thistle roots. The unfortunate man was given a pint of bear oil which reportedly relieved his intestinal distress rather quickly. When strong enough to talk, Everts told Jack Baronett his story. He essentially had retraced the Washburn party's steps, building fires with an opera glass lens and from a burning brand.

George L. Henderson, a park assistant superintendent who arrived in Yellowstone in 1882, found Jack Baronett still in the park and was thus the recipient of still another version of what Everts was like when he was found.[10] Fortunately for posterity, Henderson handwrote into one of his notebooks what Baronett said to him about Everts:

He informed his [rescuers] that he had spent two days in attempting to capture a toad for food. Mr. B[aronett] regarded this as the ravings of a maniac. When found he muttered as if to himself. They gave him a spoonful of hot tea, and small portions of venison. . . . His feet were naked, his clothes torn to shreds and one foot was worn to the bone. Portions of his body were seared and black [and] his fingers were like charred wood. . . . They

found him about 15 miles from M H Spr[ings]
in the divide between big Black Tail Creek
and Tower Creek on a right bleake mt. They
[then] moved about 3 or 4 miles per day 2d
day to Turkey Pen Creek about 11 miles [illeg-
ible] Baronett camped this first day on his
right. He [Everts] could not weigh [more than]
about 40 to 50 lbs. [Second] day [they] took him
in[to] the house. There they remained 10 days
to recuperate. . . . [He was] Found on [the]
forenoon of [the] 38th day and got to Fort Ellis
[after] about 18 days more.[11]

Samuel Langhorne, who interviewed Everts after his ordeal, had the following to say about how
he was recovering some ten days after his rescue:

It is a great pleasure to hear him talk, and he
tells you so many little incidents that you cannot remember one half of them. His condition
now is good, sound in mind, hearty in appetite,
with good digestion, and as jolly as can be; con-
verses freely and pleasantly with all who come
to see him, and is delighted with company. He
is very spare, not weighing more than eighty
pounds, but is gaining rapidly. One arm was
paralysed [sic], but is gaining action. One foot is
worn to the bone, on the outside joint, near the
little toe. He will remain here until entirely re-
cuperated, and no pains will be spared to make
him comfortable.[12]

According to a newspaper article,[13] Judge
Lawrence of Helena (the law partner of another

11. G.L. Henderson in bound volume
141, p. 100, YNP Archives.

12. "The Lost and Found," Helena *Daily
Herald*, October 28, 1870.

13. "The Lost Man. $600 Reward Of-
fered," Helena *Daily Herald*, October 6,
1870.

expedition member) had offered a $600 reward for the finding of Everts, but apparently backed out of paying it. Everts certainly owed his life to his rescuers, but Jack Baronett was later to state,

> His friends refused to pay me because I found him alive, they saying that it was his place to pay the bills. [And then] He would not pay me because he said that if I had left him alone he would have found his way out.

Moreover, when Baronett called on Everts a few years later in New York, he was received so coldly by his rescuee that the mountaineer disgustedly commented to others that "he wished he had let the son-of-a-gun roam."[14]

TODAY A LONG, high ridge just east of Mammoth Hot Springs bears the name of Mount Everts, and a creek on its eastern side is called Rescue Creek. General H.D. Washburn transferred the name Mount Everts to this present location through a misunderstanding as to where Everts was found. The error was made worse when the Hayden survey changed the name of nearby "Lost Trail Creek" to Rescue Creek, also on the assumption that Everts was found there.[15]

The original "Mount Everts," south of the Southeast Arm of Yellowstone Lake, is the north end of present Two Ocean Plateau, and the mountain that Everts himself called "Mount Everts" is today known as Mount Sheridan.

14. Baronett in Gerrish, p. 240; R.C. Wallace, *A Few Memories of a Long Life* (privately printed, 1900), p. 61.

15. Map of Washburn in Langford, "The Wonders of the Yellowstone," *Scribner's Monthly* 2:3, May, 1871; Henry Gannett, 1878 map of whole park in F.V. Hayden, *12th Annual Report . . .* , pt. II (Washington: GPO, 1883). Two newspaper articles in the Helena *Daily Herald* (October 21, 26, 1870) added to the confusion by stating that Everts was found "near the mouth of Bear Gulch," which is about fifteen miles too far northwest.

As for the actual spot where Everts was found, it has long been associated with a misunderstanding. As mentioned, Mount Everts and Rescue Creek were named because Everts's rescue site was wrongly thought to be just east of present Mammoth Hot Springs, whereas the actual rescue location was on the west slopes of Crescent Hill just east of the canyon known as the Cut. The confusion between the two locations (which are about nine or ten miles apart) was because both Gardner River and Tower Creek had been called "Warm Spring Creek" by 1860s prospectors. Thus, when Baronett's rescue location was reported in newspapers as "on the summit of the first big mountain beyond Warm Spring Creek," Dr. F.V. Hayden and Henry Washburn each assumed the site to be just east of Gardner River rather than at the Crescent Hill location west of Tower Creek.[16]

Historian Hiram Chittenden reported Everts's true rescue spot in 1895 in a letter to the park superintendent, and he wanted the site marked in some way:

> By the way I got an interesting item from Barronett [sic] lately. It was he, you know, who found Everts. I was surprised to learn that he found him over near the 'Devil's Cut' (or 'Gut') and not on Mt. Everts at all. He says he piled up a mound of stones where he found him. I find this statement confirmed by Norris who visited the spot when he was Supt. If this is a fact, and if that mark is still there, I believe it would be a good idea to perpetuate it. Everts'

16. "The Long-Lost Found," in Helena *Daily Herald*, October 21, 1870; Haines, "Lost in the Yellowstone," *Montana Magazine of Western History* 22:41, Summer, 1972; Haines, *The Yellowstone Story*, I, pp. 113, 144.

adventure was really a most singular one and there are a good many curious features about it that are quite inexplicable. I think it is going to be one of the most important episodes in the history of the Park and I believe it would be a good idea to preserve this monument, if it is a fact that Baronett [placed] one there.[17]

Unfortunately for posterity, Chittenden's suggestion to mark the exact rescue spot was ignored. The pile of rocks that Baronett erected came to be called the "Baronett-Everts Cairn," but the spot was lost for all time when Jack Baronett and Truman Everts both died in 1901. Historian Aubrey Haines, who searched hard for the spot, says that at this date no one can go to a specific pile of rocks and say that it is the Baronett-Everts Cairn. There are several possible piles of rock there, some natural and some possibly Indian manhood-site piles. All we know is that the spot was on the west slope of Crescent Hill, not far from where the present road (the Bannock Trail in 1870) enters the Cut, and east of the present road.[18]

Everts was first choice in 1872 when it came time to pick a superintendent for the newly created Yellowstone National Park, a result of the public's interest caused by his magazine article. About this Everts wrote later to his friend Norris: "I hope there is some pay attached to [your superintendency]. When I was an applicant for the position there was no appropriation to pay such an officer and I could not afford to take it solely for the honor tho[ugh] I wanted to very much."[19] So

17. Chittenden to George S. Anderson, March 28, 1895, Archive Document 2243, YNP Archives.

18. Park photographer Jack Haynes, who spent his entire life in Yellowstone, had a different (and incorrect) location for the Everts rescue site that we mention here in order to complete the record. In the fall of 1937, Haynes and park superintendent E.B. Rogers set out to find the site. From "contemporary newspaper accounts" (all of them used here) and "a remark by Major Chittenden" (quoted above), it was, according to Haynes and Rogers,

> quite certain that the spot was ten [sic] miles east of Mammoth and not far from the old Bannock trail. Several square miles were examined in detail and on foot in attempting to find it. Rogers and Haynes were rewarded by finding a considerable mound of man laid rocks (somewhat tumbled down and 6 by 8 feet across) on a rounded hill in the range of the meager description of it, with no other possible cairn within a radius of several miles.

("Baronett-Everts Cairn" in Yellowstone Card File, Park Museum Curator's office) Haynes responded by placing a description of this cairn in the text of his *Haynes Guide to Yellowstone Park* and showing the site on a map (see for example the 1966 edition, pp. 158, 163). However, historian Aubrey Haines says Jack Haynes erred in placing the location here, and indeed, the 1895 Chittenden letter places the site closer to the Cut and not so far west as Haynes and Rogers placed it. Aubrey L. Haines to Doris Whithorn, October 20, 1994, in possession of author.

19. Everts to P.W. Norris, April 21, 1877, in National Archives, RG 48, no. 62, roll 1; hard copy at YNP Library.

the position went to his fellow expeditioner N.P. Langford. Thus, according to historian Aubrey L. Haines, "his fame rests solely on that wilderness ordeal when it might well have been tied in with the opening years of our first national park." Nevertheless, Everts's ordeal lent great publicity and support to that burgeoning movement which led to the establishment of Yellowstone.[20]

It is well known that Truman Everts returned for a visit to the Yellowstone country many years later with his daughter Bessie.[21] Not as well known is P.W. Norris's claim that Everts visited Yellowstone Park again only two years later in 1872, for Norris was preparing that trip journal by Everts for publication with Norris's other notes when Norris died in 1885. According to Norris, Everts, after his Yellowstone adventure, had charge of Rockcastle Springs, Kentucky, as some sort of park administrator, for Norris stated that Everts's "pressing duties . . . in fitting his Rockcastle (Ky.) Springs for Centennial Visitors" in 1876 prevented the publication of that second Everts journal by Norris.[22] And, letters to Norris from Everts, mailed from that place in Kentucky, show that Norris prevailed upon his old friend Everts to accompany him to Yellowstone in 1877 to begin Norris's park superintendency. After planning for some time to go, Everts finally wrote to Norris that his weak financial condition prevented it: "This grieves me much as there is nothing that could give me greater pleasure than to be your companion among the mountains."[23]

Everts was to have one more round with Yellowstone. Correspondence from Everts to the Sec-

20. Aubrey L. Haines, "Lost in the Yellowstone," p. 41.

21. William W. Wylie, (Yellowstone National Park History and Reminiscences of his days there), ms. prepared in 1926, and original donated to YNP Library, p. 2.

22. Norris, "Meanderings . . . ," letter #46, note *A*.

23. Everts to P.W. Norris, April 26, 1877, in National Archives, RG 48, no. 62, roll 1; hard copy at YNP Library.

24. T.C. Everts to Appointment Clerk, September 8, 1885, in NA, RG 48, no. 62, roll 4 (hardcopy at YNP Library). In this letter, Everts stated: "Please let Mr. C[owan?] have the papers I filed with you asking for the appointment of superintendent Yellowstone National Park."

25. About his interview with Truman Everts, Jr., and the original Everts manuscript, Historian Aubrey Haines says,

Years ago [1961] I attempted to get more info on Everts from his son, Truman, Jr., then a very old man. I talked with him while touring him about the Park one day, and he promised to send the Park some Everts papers, including the handwritten MS of the *Scribner's* article. He went back to New York and moved his residence to Florida. In the course of the move, his father's papers were destroyed (his statement when I followed up on his promise. I do not know if he was truthful in this, or merely avoiding his earlier promise). All I was able to get directly from Truman, Jr., has been included in *The Yellowstone Story*, II, p. 433.

Haines to Tom Tankersley, October 17, 1994.

retary of the Interior in 1885 indicates that Everts apparently applied unsuccessfully that year for the superintendency of Yellowstone. By then the position was a paid one.[24]

In 1961, Everts's son Truman Everts, Jr., walked into Yellowstone Park headquarters at Mammoth Hot Springs and consented to an interview with park historian Aubrey Haines, thus increasing our knowledge of the Everts family. The young Everts had been only nine years old when his father died, but possessed some knowledge of the elder Everts. He stated that his father met his second wife (the younger Everts's mother) in Washington, D.C., and married her sometime in 1880-81. The elder Everts lived in Toledo, Ohio before moving to Washington, D.C., where he worked for the U.S. Post Office. Truman Everts, Jr., remembered his mother saying that the family had hard times during the Cleveland administrations because they were of the wrong political party.[25]

Truman Everts senior died of pneumonia at Hyattsville, Maryland, on February 16, 1901, and was buried in Glenwood Cemetery. His wife died in 1947, and was also buried there.

Everts's published account of his adventures stimulated interest in the Washburn Expedition and in the marvelous Yellowstone country which they helped discover. That interest helped make Yellowstone the world's first national park in 1872.

Lost in the Yellowstone

The Handwritten
Records of
Truman C. Everts

An Interview in 1996 with Everts's Granddaughter Helen Margaret Evarts Banks

O<small>N</small> J<small>UNE</small> 27, 1996, thirty-five years after park historian Aubrey Haines interviewed her father, the granddaughter of Truman C. Everts came to Mammoth Hot Springs in Yellowstone National Park to meet with me in my position as then Park archivist. We had set up this appointment by telephone several months earlier. Helen Margaret Evarts Banks, age 76, was born in 1920. With her were her daughter, Mary Elena Fillback Widger (a great-granddaughter of Truman C. Everts), and her daughter's two children. I inscribed copies of my book *Lost in the Yellowstone* to each of them in a way that acknowledged their relationship to their forebear.

With me during the interview with Mrs. Banks were my summer assistants, Scott Hanley and Mike Stevens. The three of us talked with her for some two and one-half hours and learned that she had brought with her several handwritten documents that Truman Everts wrote sometime before he died in 1901. These were the documents that historian Aubrey Haines learned about in 1961 at the time he interviewed Mrs. Banks's father, Truman Evarts Jr. Evarts had promised to send those documents to Haines and the park at that time, but later told Haines that he had lost the documents when he moved from New York to

Florida. The documents had in fact remained with the Everts descendants until this summer day in 1996.

When I told Mrs. Banks the story involving her father, she reiterated that her father had possessed the documents all the time, but that he simply did not want anyone else to have them, for whatever reasons.

Mrs. Banks provided the park with a newspaper obituary of Truman Everts's second wife (and the grandmother of Mrs. Banks), Imogene S. Everts Moore. After Truman C. Everts died in 1901, Imogene married William H. Moore in 1908; she died in 1949 in Washington, D.C. Imogene and Mr. Moore had no children together, although Imogene had had one child with Truman C. Everts, Helen Banks's father, Truman C. Evarts Jr., who married Mary Agnes McNulty. We noted differences in the spelling of the last name, which Mrs. Banks would soon explain to us.

Mrs. Banks was quite forthcoming in her responses to our questions about her father and grandmother. I asked her whether her grandmother Imogene Moore (who lived until her granddaughter was twenty-nine) ever mentioned Truman C. Everts. She replied, "I always thought that she never got over him." When I asked why, she stated that it was simply that her grandmother's attitude seemed one of adoration, adding that "she doted on my father so much." Asked whether or not her father ever talked of his mother, she stated: "He used to say that his mother 'would not tell me anything about her life.'"

Mrs. Banks told us some other things about her grandmother Imogene. Concerning Truman C. Everts's death: "Grandmother said he worked [in his last years] in a new building [in Washington] and that the plaster wasn't dry there and that he caught a cold from it and died [in 1901]." Concerning Truman Everts's injury in Yellowstone, she stated: "My father said he always remembered the scars on his father's back from [his] sleeping by the hot springs."

From Mrs. Banks's family documents and her memory, we were able to reconstruct information about the spelling of the name *Everts* or *Evarts*. Truman C. Everts's signature spelled the name with a central "e" (see the photo reproduced in this book and in Langford's 1905 diary), but family documents that Mrs. Banks brought with her indicate that Truman's son (Truman C. Evarts Jr.) and Truman's father (William Evarts) both spelled the name with a central "a." It thus appears that the idiosyncratic change to "e" occurred *only* with Truman C. Everts himself and did not apply to either his father or his son. (Even Everts's handwritten document at one point spells "Mt. Evarts" with the central "a," a curious inconsistency considering that his known signature uses an "e.")

Mrs. Banks gave us as much provenance for Truman C. Everts's handwritten documents as she knew. She stated that her father, Truman C. Evarts Jr., always kept them "in a black tin box" and that he was very stingy with them. "He wasn't going to part with those [papers]," she stated. "He was very protective of them." When I asked Mrs. Banks whether her father ever said anything to her about the documents, she stated: "He just said don't ever let anybody have these documents."

According to Mrs. Banks, her father died in 1972. Twenty-four years later, she allowed the park to make copies of the family documents, but she would not donate the originals. She explained to us that her daughter and grandchildren objected to any plan to give away the originals.

THE DOCUMENTS

Mrs. Banks provided the park with copies of four different handwritten documents, copies that today repose in the Yellowstone National Park Library. One of those documents proved to be Truman C. Everts's handwritten account of his adventures while lost in Yellowstone in 1870. It is an incredibly valuable, primary source document that we reproduce here in its entirety.

Two other documents are also handwritten, but do not seem to relate to either Yellowstone National Park or Truman Everts himself, so they are omitted here. The fourth document is a brief handwritten autobiography penned by Everts. A transcription of this memoir follows, with all spelling and punctuation anomalies intact; it adds a great deal of material to the little that we have known about Truman C. Everts's life before 1864. These documents were placed in the Yellowstone National Park Research Library in 1996.

Both the Everts autobiography and his handwritten account of being lost in the Yellowstone in 1870 are published for the first time in this book. My editorial method has been to present the spellings and order of words exactly as Truman Everts wrote them, but to suggest a word in square brackets when Everts's manuscript was illegible.

Autobiography of Truman C. Everts

[begin page marked 1]

My Grandfather Evarts was in the war of the Revolution, and for a time was engaged in [*illegible*] and brot some [*illegible*] in to the harbor of New London [Connecticut], which were burned by the traitor Arnold when he burnt New London.

My Mother was a Bishop from Conn, My Father was Wm Evarts a farmer from Bolton Vt. and was the most influential man of that part of the state, was elected to Legislator whenever he desired to be, was a U.S. Custom house office and, wealthy, as men were rated at that time[.] he had 13 children I was next to the youngest—He was a soldier in the war of 1812 as well as his eldest son Horatio.

I was born May 30, 1816 at Boltin [*sic*] [Vermont.] My Father when I was 6 years old moved to Burlington Vt

[begin page marked 2]

where I resided until I was 13 years old. at which time my Father was involved in financial difficulties, by his desire to help others, and could never refuse to assist those who asked him, and was finally ruined by his kindness, when he said to me He had intend that I should have had a Collegiate Education, and I had been preparing for it by attending Academy at Willerton[?], but his finacial condition made it impossible for him to do so, and that this was an opportunity for me to go with a gentleman to Buffalo NY. or I might take a position in a store in Burlington[.] I decided to go to Buffalo as I had a desire to see the world/ an unfortunate decision for a boy of my age 1830 [age 14]—I remained in Buffalo

[begin page marked 3]
about two years then went to Cleveland Ohio and about two years when I returned to Vt. and spent the winter, but returned to Buffalo and took a positon on a Steam Boat running to Detroit[.] as the winter stopped navigation I went to Huron with Capt Walker who comanded the Boat I saild on—and as there was no work I worked at ship building on the Steam Boat Columbus and saild on her the next season and in the fall of that year 1834 went to Toledo ohio (then Virtula) and work as clerk in hotel[.] the next year I was offered a clerkship in the Post Office by E D Potter who was the pm [postmaster.] I remaind 15 years, when by a vote of the

[begin page marked 4]
people I was made Postmaster which I held 5 years as it was a first class office[.] I receid two thousand dollars a year with the box rents amounted more than $3500 during which time I was elected an alderman and other local office[.] during all these years I never to my knowledge [had] an enemy being one of the most popular young men of the city[.] in 1849 I

married a Miss Morrison of Dayton[.] this proved to be an unfortunate marriage—I was in 1851 offered the Depty of the PO at Chicago at $2200 which I held until the [election.?] between Senator Douglas and President Buchanan, and Alsa[?] Price the PM who was Mr. Douglas friend, was removed, and I regained my position and went to Louisville Ky and went into Partnership with my Brother a merchant in that city[.]

[begin page marked 5]

I remained there until the rebellion when I was ordered to leave by rebels, when I came to Washington to get permission to raise a Rgt [regiment] of Union solder but at that time Ky was neutral or said so and [I] could do nothing—I remained in Washington until the 1st Battle of Bull Run when I joined the first NJ Rgt under Col. Ruifin[?] and went to that Battle. The ex[haustion.?] of that day and night brot on the infliction reh[eumatism.?] and I was laid up for months, and when I came back there was no opportunity for me to get back into the Service in a position[?] I was in a condition to take, and being offered a position in the [Treasury?] Dept where I remained until 1864 when on the organization of the Territory of Montana President Lincoln offered me the Assessor of Internal Revenue which I accepted.

[begin unmarked page 6]

I held the office 6 years to the satisfaction to the government and the people having the reputation of being one of the most efficient officers in the revenue service.

In the year 1870 I help organize an expedition to explore the unknown sources of the Yellow Stone river[.] Many attemps had been made by the military and by [*illegible*—citizens?] to this unknown region but none secedd, but two [three] gentmen of the Territory got into what is know as the [National] Park the previous year as far as the Yellow Stone Fall and gave wonderfuld account of what they saw—Our expeditio was composed 6 citizens and 7 soldis from Fort Ellis[.] we chose Gen Washburn of the Land Office capt of the expeditin, we left Helena July in a snow storm[.] when we arrived at Fort Ellis

[begin unmarked page 7]
the weather was very pleasant but when we arrived at the Yellowstone Valley we found snow again after which we had very pleasant weather until sept[.] we had a Very great difficulty in getting to the Falls as we had to pass over a range of Mountains without any knowledge of the country but finally found a deer trail and followed over the mountain into the valy of the Yellow Stone Lake at the Great Falls of the Yellowstone now so well described by the tourist that has since travelled over the route, and stages where we had to get along with great difficulty on horseback. Went to the Lake and around the southern end of the Lake[.] When the
party left the lake on west [*sic*—south] end of the Lake, on that day while leadg the party in trying to find a place

[begin page marked "8"]
to cover the peninsula my horse got into a big Hole and with much difficulty I extricated him but in doing so I [*illegible*] the trail of the party which had gone on before, and startd on a trail which I suppose

was the one one party had taken, but not coming up to them I thought there was something wrong and on examing the trail I found it was a deer trail, as it was then near night I gave up hope of finding my party that night and coming to a small opening in the forest I concluded to spend the night there and fastning my horse I unsadled him and had to make a fire but as I had no matches I tried to make a with my Pistol but did not su[ccee]d and cralled under a fallen tree rested until morning[.]

[Here ends the handwritten autobiography of Truman C. Everts.]

Preface to Everts's Handwritten Account

The second important Everts document given to Yellowstone National Park on June 27, 1996, is a handwritten account numbering twenty-eight (including small pages). Some of the pages are numbered and some are not, but the story seems complete. On the reverse of page six, someone has stamped a name with a commercial inkpad stamp that reads: "T.C. Evarts," spelled with a central "a."

This handwritten account is not the same as the one Everts published in *Scribner's Monthly* and it adds some details not in that published account. I have no way of knowing when it was written, but it is possible that it represents Everts's first attempt at a narrative after he returned from his adventure. Perhaps it was used to prepare his Scribner's account or perhaps it was written later; we simply do not know those particulars. However, it is apparent that he wrote it not earlier than the year following his 1870 adventure, as a reference in it states that a mountain in the national park is called "Mt. Evarts." That naming occurred in 1871.

The manuscript's inconsistent pagination and the fact that it was written on several different sizes of paper scraps give the impression that some pages may be missing, although the story seems chronologically and narratively complete. As Mrs. Banks presented them to us, the original pages were in haphazard order In transcribing them, I have rearranged them into a logical chronological order, which is reflected here. However, any researcher can note the page numbering that Everts (or perhaps someone else) placed at the top of many of the original pages, as I have faithfully reproduced those page numbers. The following transcription keeps all spelling and punctuation intact. Brackets indicate my emendations.

Everts's Handwritten Account of Being Lost in the Yellowstone

[Begin page marked 1]

1st night after seperating from party my horse got into mire[?] hole and with great difficulty I got him out[.] this near night and being anxious to overtake the party before dark I took a trail which I urged my horse as fast as possible through a dense forest until I thought I ought to be up with the party. I got off my horse to reconnoiter [?] and on examining the trail found I was not on the trail of the party but on an Elk trail. I then [had] nothing to do but to follow it, and just before dark came into an opening of fallen timber. I found it impossible to go further and took my traps[?] of my horse and [secured?] him for the night and tried make a fire[.] as I had no matches put powder and paper into my Pistol[?] and tried to ignite the paper but could not succeed and gave up the effort[.] made a pillow of my saddle and covered myself with the saddle blanket—I laid down for night. It was impossible to sleep and the breaking of brush and twigs in the [forest? first?] alarmed me as I thought it must be a bear or lion and did not know when it might attack me—as soon as light I saddled my horse and it being a very difficult place to extricate myself and horse from—I left my horse to find the best place to get out—I had but a short distance when I heard my [horse]

[begin page marked 2]

gave a shriek and bounded off like a deer over the fallen timber—that was the last I ever saw of him[.] he had undoubtedly seen a bear, which made him [cower?] as a horse have great fear of that animal. I was left without any thing but my opera glass an knife[.] my gun pistol blanket & [*word missing*] was gone—It was a trying moment—but there was only one thing to be done find my party on foot[.] after putting up a notice that if any of the party came to that place to wait for me until the next day telling them the direction I had gone—hoping to find the party during the day—I follow a small stream until nea night and not finding the party I tried to [return?] to where I left my notes in the morning—night coming I found a fallen spruce tree with the foilege still on it—I [c]rawled under it for the nigh—I was taken very seriously ill during the night and was much exhed by throwing from my stomach all that was in it—about noon I found my notice but no one had been there[.] I felt then that I was really lost—exming the country about I found tracks of my horse who had [covered?] my track in my absence—but I saw nothing of him[.]

[begin page marked 3]

the next day I took my dirction towards a lake I had seen from the mountain I was on and started on my travels again[.] about noon I sat down to rest on a log and feeling the knawings of hunger I looked about to discover something eatable[.] there was a thistle gwing at my feet[.] I took my knife and dug up the root—and tasted it[.] it did not seem of have any nouristrut in[.] in fact almost tasteless—but I eat some of it and after eating a while I put up my knife in its sheath attached to my belt as I supposed and started again[.] after a few hours I stopped eat again and wanting my knife put my hand in the sheath to get it[.] alas found it gone[.] what a loss[!] it was all I had to defend myself or to procure food[.] I felt it keenly[.] it was no use to look for it as I had come miles from when I lost it and I could not have found the way back to it—I so started again with a heavy heart[.] that night under some fir trees I dug with my hands a hole and gathered le[a] ve[s] and brush to keep from freezing my feet—but not fuly safe from wild beast scalded a tree near by which I could

[begin page marked 4]

climb in case of danger[.] It was fortunate that I did so—as I had not laid down but a short time before I heard in the dirtion the breaking of twigs and brush which I was sure was some

animal[.] I did not have to wait long to be sure that it was a lion as I heard a low growling as he came near[.] I assure you I lost no time in getting to the tree and getting up, and I had no more than got out of his reach before he was under the tree—my [*illegible*] was anything but agreeable [and] though I could not see him madde his prsence known by continual growling going around the tree debating I suppose whether it was prudent to come up to me or not[.] I kept up shouting[.] this lasted for some time[.] I getting very cold and calculating how long I could hold out[.] at last after perhaps 30 minutes he [*illegible*—seemed?] to [*illegible*—pause?l] and consider[.] I doubt whether he had ever come in contact with the human voice before and it was a mysterious sound to him[.] he was silent for a minute or two[.] I thought he was preparing for a leap into the tree and thought my time was about out—but I was relieved from this terrible stress by hearing him

[begin an unnumbered page]

Breaking brush and growling[.] His sound kept becoming more distant until I could not hear him— Nearly pershid by the cold I could not have retained my position only latter longer so taking the chances of his not returning I came down from the bed I had made and crawled into [*word omitted*] so exausted as to have lost all fear and dropped off to sleep and did not awake until daylight[.] It was a terrible night— Nothing to eat[.] I walked along about ready to give up[.] about noon of this day a heavy blinding snow storm came on and finding a fir tree whose foilege was so dense as to shelter me from the snow I rested under it—looking out I saw a little snow bird that had got so wet that he could not fly[.] I started in chase of him and caught him in a snow bank[.] I took his feathers off very quickly and soon eat him and proved to be a delicious morsel the first food I had had for 3 day except a taste of thistle root[.] Under this tree I stayed until the storm abated & next

[begin page marked 30 [illegible] page [illegible] at top]

about dark came to the Lake [Heart Lake.] there were many hot springs & geysers around it[.] I laid down on the hot crust that surround the springs to get warm and passed the night—but during the night the crust broke through and let out the hot steam and burned me severly—The next day looking around I found a boiling spring with a grassy margin—and as I could go no further in my weaknd condition decide to make it my final resting place and getting some stick and bough of pine I made me a house over the spring sloping it over so as to catch the hot steam and keep me warm—here I found more thistles and digging up th roots with my hands I took into the shelter and crawled in with th[em?] the roots into the b[*illegible*—bough house?] with they would cook and with a sick[.]

[begin page marked 21; one or more pages may be missing here]

Under this bough house I passed 12 days and nights thoroughly wet by the hot steam—eating of scanty supply of thistle roots—One morning a band of Elks came around my spring the males on one side and a band of females on the other[.] the male was the finest specimen of animal life I ever saw full six feet in height[.] with antlers spreading fully first[?] across he was prading himself before his harem to the greatest advantage[.] they were seemed to fill them with greatest admiration—their heads erect and every[?] [*illegible*—hair?] out from the head and their eyes stretched to their utmost—the whole scene was most beautiful display of Elk life—during this season of the year the Elk chooses his herd or family with which he allows no interference which is the occasion of many fearful battles between these monarchs of the mountains—oh! how I wished for my rifle or Pistol as they were within a few feet of me an unconcious of my presence[.] I could easily got provision for a

winter [*illegible*—sitting?] here without any hope of
getting away as the snow upon the mountains and in
the Valeys made it impossible for me to travel as I had
no way as I supposed of making fire without which
I could not live as the night was cold to freising and
ice[?] I thought I could make this my final resting place
survive as long as I could—But one day the sun shone
and with much warmth—several day of this weather
& looking up the mountain side I saw that the snow
was melting and dry earth appeard—The[n] I thought
I might get away and if I had fire this seemed a prophet
of reaching the settlements[.] I thought of any mode
that I had ever heard of making a fire that now seemed
to be available—One day I thought of a sun glass—all
I had saved from my traps was my opera glass—can I
make a fire with this[?]

[begin page marked 5]

The thought electrified and I rawled from my bed
of steam that I had lain in so many days and got into
the warm sun light took out the lens from my opera
glass and made an effort with both glasses[.] it did
not suceed[.] I was greatly disappointed[.] hope sank
within me[.] getting some dry wood from a hollow
tree I took one lense and again tried[.] oh what joy[!]
it smoked[.] I was so overcome I laid down to rest[.]
I was overcome[.] gaining strength I tried again and
after an hour of hard work I got a [blaze?][.] then
gathing all the dry twigs I piled them up and soon was
warming myself by the cheerful blase—I imedatly set
about preparing for a start for [*illegible*—liberty?][.] My
boots had been so soaked by the steam that I could no
longer get them in so making with one the buckles
on my pants I made by grinding on the stones a sharp

edge and with it after much laborer cut the tops of my boots off[.] I could then get them on—and sowing one end of the boot leg I made a pouch and gathering thistles enough to fill this and running the straps[?] on to my belt I was able to carry them without much difficulty—after a day or two of prepartion started one morning hoping to be able to make a fire to keep me warm at night—I traveled all that day and night came on I stopped in order to make a fire[.] I had a very painful day of travel and was greatly

[begin page marked 6]

fatigued with all my efforts[.] the sun went down and I could make no fire—It was very cold in a dismal[?] forest[.] I passed a dreadful night[.] I had to exercise [*illegible*—working?] myself to keep from freising[.] I dare not lie down as I might drop to sleep—and thus perish from the cold so I walked and exercised[?] my hands until morning—I could not make a fire—I had left a fire at the lake which I had left the morning[.] I thought my only cover was to get back to the fire although it was with great reluctance I did so as every hour to me then seemed days as if I was caught in another snow storm there was no hope of my getting out—I traveled back and reached the lake and fire at night[.] renewing the fire I sat down by the lake took off my shoes and found my feet so swollin and worn that I almost gave up hope—getting my feet in the cold water of the Lake I laid down by this fire and had a good night of sleep[.] I found in the morning that my feet were still so swollen that I could [not?] get on my shoes, and I had to remain [*illegible*— two days?] of the greatest anxiety—the third day I was able to get on my shoes and make another start and prepared myself with a brand of fire to carry with me that might be sure to burn [*illegible*][.]

[begin page marked 7]

I took a different route this morning up a long peninsula running to the Yellow Stone Lake[.] it took several days to reach the top and was very [*illegible—treacherous?*] as it was a dense forest and very difficult to keep the right-direction[.] I had to get a tree in the direction I wanted to go and keep it in sight until I reached it and then do the same thing over[.] One night I found it very difficult to keep warm and in fuley dry fir timber I thought I might keep warm by its blaze so setting fire to it—it burned so fiercely and the heat was so intense that I had to get so far from it that my back would be cold and my face too hot so I was compelled to go away from it and build me a little fire and get over it—The Indian mod[e][.] they never make a large fire but a small one that they can get near to it and be more comfortable[.] I after this experience adopted their plan and made no more large fires[.] the fourth day I start down the mountain and came to the lake shore[.] I was very much exhasted and my shoes became very painful to my feet from the high heels which turned over and I found it necessary to get the heels off and at night I undertook the job which proved to be a long and troublesom affair—the only tools I had was a sharp stick[?] and I was nearly all night in doing it and thus[?] found[?] that I had lowered the soles and had to tie this on my feet with strips of bark—the next day I reach a camp where my party had camped on their way home[.] I felt sure that I should find something that had been left for me to eat If I happened to come here—but after searching

eny place that seemed likely that they would leave it
I found nothing to eat but found a fork and a yeast
powder can which proved of service and used this to
boil my roots and to dig them[.]

[begin page marked 8]

as they left some bough tents to sleep in I thought
by occupying on or thru[?] them I should have a good
nights rest and gathering all the pine boughs I could
and making a small fire laid down to rest—but I was
not to have so much comfort for in the night came
up a strong wind and before I could help myself this
fire was blown into my brush and set it on fire and
with difficulty I escaped without getting burned—I
left without a fire and very cold wind blowing[.] no
shelter[?] and was obliged wander about all night to
keep from freising—I provd a serious loss to me as
I had made from unraveling my handkerchief a fish
line and made a hook out of my gold frame eyeglasses
with much trouble and time and they were burned
up so my hope of appeasing my hunger with fish was
gone—the snow ~~must have been~~ ^was^ on the ground
when they were her and I found the direction this to
by the track of their horses—I though in following
their trail I should come out all right but after two days
travel the snow having disappeared I could no longer
follow them[.] I did not know which way to go—after
deliberating some time I was afraid to venture further
on that course[.] The[?] only course was to get back
to the Lake and follow that to where the party struck
on our way out—with a sad heart I turned back
having lost several days of great importance to me for
if another snow storm came there was no chance of
my getting out—the next day I reached the lake very

much worn[?] out having been out of roots for several days[.] this night I came to a [three words illegible] tree[?] on the margin of the Lake with a large hollow in it[.]

[begin page marked 9]

looking into it it seemed to be the home of a bear but I [it?] look so comfortable I thought I would [*illegible*—sleep in?] it one night at the risk of coming into contact with the owner[.] all around was dry fallen timber and knowg that wild animals were avers to fire I gathered all the dry wood I could get around the opening in the tree and then setting fire to the falling trees around I crawled in to the hole and set fire to the dry sticks I gathered before the opening res[*illegible*—reserving?] in side enough to replenish the fire in the night[.] I went to sleep and had the best night rest I had during all my wanderings—I started early in the morning—and in giving over to the shore of the Lake I was greatly startled by discovering in the sand the track of a bear the largest one I ever saw[.] It must have been a very large grizzly and I [*illegible*—presumed?] the owner of the bed I slept in—I got to the shore of the lake as soon as possible and got away from that place as soon as possible and never got a sight of the animal[.] Next day discovered the [*illegible*—form?] of a bird on the shore with some flesh on it[.] I broke it up and started a fire and in my yeast can made a soup of water & bones[.] there was very little or no nourishment in it but drank it and was thankful[.] for several days I could find no roots and so I went hungry—during the day I became very thirsty and [*illegible*] coming to a small stream that was down in a ravine [begin page marked with 22(?)]

at least 100 feet and very abrupt but my thirst was so great that I had to get to it[.]   sliding down to this stream was very t[*illegible*—treacherous? terrible?] but the water very fine—and after quenching my thirst and resting I started to get out[.] I found I had made a mistake for it took me nearly a half day to climb out[.] I was completely exhausted and my thirst was greater than befor I went down[.] I never tried the experiment again but made snow into balls and carried them in my pocket[.]

[begin a second page marked 9]

three days travel brot me to the south [*sic*—west] end of the Lake where I got in to the trail of our party when we were going into the Park and near the great falls. here I camped & found a piece of c[*illegible*—cord?] left by the party—all night I worked at unravelling it and made another fish line and taking the buckles off my pants made a hook of it hoping when I reached the river below the grand canyon where we caught many trout I might be able to get some with which I then thought I could have strength enough to get to the ranch of my friends the Boettlers who ranching about as I estimated about 30 miles from the great falls—my next days journey brot me to the falls where the country was somewhat familiar to me as I spent two days—all these many days of travel I had during the day carried a brand and each night had no difficulty in making fire but today it went out and [I] stopped about the middle of the afternoon to try to get fire with my glass but not being able to get dry wood after working until the sun went down I was not able to make a fire[.] it was very cold—Seeking for a sheltered place I went into the woods but I did not find any place that I could keep warm and to keep from freesing I walked around exercising with hand & feet until morning—when I with great effort was able to get to a small opening in woods where the sun shone—when I fell [*illegible*—unconscious?] and [*illegible*] so for [*sic*—for so] many hours when I came to my sense it was midday and in making an effort to get up I found my right arm

[begin page marked 10]

arm paralyzed and hanging useless by my side[.] It was a dreadful affliction as this arm done the most of my work and particularly making fire as it required much steadiness to

hold the glass to get it in proper focus—but by putting the lens into the hand and holding it with the[?] other I was enabled to get a fire. And had bitter night[?][.] in fact I thought I should have to give up— The range of mountains boding the river we passed on our coming into this valley[.] we came over on an Elk trail which was very distinct until we reached the summit when it branched in all directions—I had to find their trail & could only do so by following the crest of these mountains which took me two days of toil to do so—In m[arching?] I had c[hosen?] a very s[teep?] grassy slope and when at the top was completely exhausted and lying down unbuckled my belt to [*two words illegible*] to which I al[*illegible*—also?] attached my glass[.] after resting a long time I t[urned?] my belt around and pursued my search for the trail[.] worn out I stopped to make a fire and prepare[?] for the night[.] on looking for my glass oh horror I could not find[.] I could [not?] live another night without them when I could no longer make a fire[.] I could go no farther in all my wanderings I had never felt such a terrible condition[.] what could I do[?] how could I find [them?] I had come over r[*illegible*—rugged?] spires[?] of mountains & crossed streams[.] where had I lost them[?] now was it possible to find them[?]—I thought over the day travel and finally that I must have left them on the m[ountain?] [where] I

[begin unnumbered page]

I laid down to rest in the morning[.] I at once [took] to the backward track with little hope but in desperation and imposing on my mind the route I came as well as I could[.] with [*illegible*—weary?] steps I searched for the grassy slope[.] after of several hours of terrible suffering I came to what I thought to be the place—and began to look for the place I laid dow and oh, what joy what rapture[?] I saw my glasses[.] I was saved[!] I could [go] no further[.] getting[?] a [*two words illegible*] was able to make a fire before the sun went down and laid very tired but so [*illegible*—happy?] that I had a good nights rest[.] The next day I found the trail that led over the mountain near what is now know as Mt Washburn[.] I was buoyed up with the hope that the next day I should get to the place where I hoped to catch fish to carry me to safety [*illegible*]—near night—the 5 day I arrived at the place know as the [*two words illegible*—blackfeet country?] of the Yellowstone river—making fire and leaving it I diceded into the canyon and to the river[.] it was so near night that I could get no grasshopper the only bait to be had & making a large fire of driftwood laid down to wait for the morning[?] to catch my fish and go on my journey—it was a f[*illegible*—fine?] cold night and ice was made—the sun came out and I went in search of bait[.] Searched diligently until afternoon before I found a grasshopper putting[?] it on my hook I cast my line in but alas no fish when they were plenty[?]

[begin page marked 11]

when I we finsd when our party was going into the Park there was none[.] I tried every place where[?] meat[?] ought to be and got no bite[.] I could stand it no longer[.] I could [not] stay in this dismal hole longer and hastily gathering some thistle roots which were growing there I climbed up the steep canyon and at dark found the fire I left the night before[.] gathering more wood reviving the fire I laid greatly discouraged[.] I expecting another snow storm I was anxious to go on my journey and at early light crossing a stream called now the [*word omitted*] on some logs with great peril in my weak condition I made a fair days travel on ground that I recognized as passing on my way up—with the greatest difficulty I got a fire just as the sun was setting—the brand I carried all day went out the sun almost down—but there was little wood to be procured[.] I laid down with some fire it would not last till morning—I awoke in the night and found it nearly out[.] hastily gathering the few brands I crossed a small stream found a fir stick putting together[?], I kindled a blaze[.] as it was very dark I was obliged to crawl around on my hands & knees to gether enough wood from hillsid to keep my fire going until morning[.] this was another terrible night for me[.]

[begin page marked 12]

and when the sun came out and gave some warmth I again in an instant became unconcious & after many hours became concious and after getting a brand of fire to carry with me that I might not again be without fire at night[.] I had gaind quite some elevation (now calld Mt Evarts) and finding some fallen timber I made a fire and stopped for the night—it was very cold and during the night there was a fall of snow—in the morning I was so I did not know which direction to take—and thought if I could get to the river about a mile away, I could see which direction the water runs[?] and get my course again—with great fatigue I got to where I could see the water and decided upon the course I ought to take—trying to come back to my fire a fierce snow storm came and I again lost my bearing and after wandering a long time I gave it up a laid down saying I can no further[?][.] I will end my journey and yet I did not like to give it up as long as there was life left—so being too weak to [walk?] I began to [roll?] down a grassy slope I was on and as it was no considerable exertion I kept rolling into c[*illegible*] enough[.] I rolled to my fire—saved again[!]

[begin small page marked 13]
the next morning the sun shone brightly and although I could walk only with the greatest difficulty felt warm to the bone[.] clothing in tattershands dreadfully burned from carrying lighted brands with nothing to eat and [*illegible—having?*] had nothing for many days as I had gotten out of the region of thistle roots—but feeling that I new the direction to take to reach my friends the Boettlers which I calculated could be more than 20 miles distant I made an other effort to get out[.] taking a brand from the fire I started but had not gone but a short distance before I was so thoroughly chilled that I stopped to make a fire—wood was not

to be had without great difficulty and after a vain effort to get a blaze I gave it up in despair—I could make no more

[begin small unmarked page on same sheet as a crude drawing of mountains by Everts]

in my exhausted condition[.] I gave it & said I will go as long as I can and let the end come—I could not get to my friends and gave up the contest[.] I was satisfied that within an other hour would end my travels[.] it was bitterly cold with a stormy wind and on a mountain top there was no hope[.] I had been so hopeful and struggled so bravely that I did not like to give up the contest but it was inevitable—but here my bone must blanch by the winter storm or be consumed by the wild beast and as I made my mind up and accepted situation and I was so weak in mind and body that did not feel all the dreadful horror of th[.]

[begin small page marked 14]

and looking around for a place in which to draw my last breath a bright ray of light came to me a light coming from sun's rays on metal[.] I look again with my dim vision[.] what was it? my first thoughts were that it was a band of [*word missing*][.] there was hope in the thought—It came nearer when there was a voice— who are you? I could only find words to say Mr. Evarts what there is left of me—then came the welcom words we are looking for me—I am freizzin[!] make a fire[!] it was two men on horseback which a friend had sent out to look for me[.] What a miraculous delirium

[begin small torn page that is also on the same sheet as the drawing by Everts] [*several words torn off*] wood made a fire and wrapping me in blankets laid me down beside it[.] getting a warmth I enquired have you anything to eat? No they replied; have you any thing to drink—I am [*illegible*] one of the men took gun and went to look for a bird or something that I could eat[.] he came back with nothing but said if we can get you down the mountain we have some flour and sugar & coffee we can get you something t[*illegible*—that?] you can eat[.] so one of them took me off [.]

[begin small page with drawing of mountains, apparently by Everts, and it may depict Rattlesnake Butte and the north end of Mt. Everts.]

[begin small page marked 16]
we reached the foot of the mountain and the found a hunters cabin and taking posesion of it and making [*illegible*] with their[?] blankets I was able to rest comfortably and they gave [illegible—sparingly?] a spoonful at a time of coffee an bit of bread—I had not had any thing but the [illegible] thistle roots for over

thirty days[.] I had not had a movement of my bowels of 35 days—I know I was in a critical condition[.] I told one of the me to get on his horse as soon as possible[.]

[begin a small page that is unmarked but which appears to belong between 16 and 17]

that evening—just after dark came a knock at the door of the cabin[.] as we were far away from any human being as we supposed it startled but we came it and the door was opened by an old grey headed man who greeted us kindly and asked why we were there— and saying he was on his way to meet a brother who had agreed to meet him at a r[*illegible*—rendezvous?] they had agreed upon somewhere in this wild [*illegible*][.]

[begin small page marked 17]

we told how we came here and the condition we were in waiting for medicine to relieve me from my great pain—he said perhaps I have something that will be what he needs[.] I killed a bear to day & saved his fat to cook with which on my saddle and going out and securing his horse for the night brot in his saddle with a large piece of bears fat tied up in a sack[.] taking frying pan he cut of about a pound of it and put it on the fire and soon had it [*illegible*] out.

[begin small page marked 18]

after it was cool enough to take into my stomack I drank it all down—it was a very sweet and palatable[.] In a few hours I was relieved and savd and when the man came back I was well except my exhaustion [*illegible*] and two days after was able to travel in an Ambulance which had been sent out by the officer at

the Fort [Ellis.] getting to my friend Boterlers I staid
all night and was much [*illegible*] by

[begin small page marked 19]

by their kind attention[.] the next day with much
difficulty we reached the Fort in a snow[*?*] storm[*?]*
there which continued several days—